THE SOVIET POLITICAL SYSTEM

THE CONTEMPORARY SOVIET UNION SERIES:
INSTITUTIONS AND POLICIES

Each volume in the Contemporary Soviet Union Series examines in detail the facts about an important aspect of Soviet rule as it has affected the Soviet citizen in the 50 years since the Bolshevik Revolution of 1917. Subjects include industry, culture, religion, agriculture, and so on. A careful examination of official Soviet material in each field provides essential basic reading for all students of Soviet affairs.

Robert Conquest is a former Research Fellow in Soviet affairs at the London School of Economics and Political Science and Senior Fellow of Columbia University's Russian Institute. His works include *Power and Policy in the U.S.S.R.*, *The Pasternak Affair: Courage of Genius*, *Common Sense about Russia*, *The Soviet Deportation of Nationalities*, and *Russia after Khrushchev*.

THE CONTEMPORARY SOVIET UNION SERIES:

INSTITUTIONS AND POLICIES

EDITED BY ROBERT CONQUEST

The Soviet
Political System

FREDERICK A. PRAEGER, *Publishers*

New York · Washington

BOOKS THAT MATTER

Published in the United States of America in 1968
by Frederick A. Praeger, Inc., Publishers
111 Fourth Avenue, New York, N.Y. 10003

Introduction © 1968 in London, England, by Robert
Conquest

Library of Congress Catalog Card Number: 68-17378

This book is Number 200 in the series
*Praeger Publications in Russian History and World
Communism*

Printed in Great Britain

Contents

Editor's Preface, 7

Editor's Preface

This book, like the others in the series, is a factual and documentary summary of its field. But, perhaps even more than the others, it requires to be put in a general perspective. For the political system is the central fact of Soviet life. And it is above all political attitudes which have been at issue in all the controversies which have become public in Russia, as in the other Communist countries, in recent years. What the intelligentsia are in effect demanding is not a change in the economic or social structure of the USSR, but a measure of civil and political liberty. The country faces economic difficulties, and resentments too, but the immediate theme of Soviet evolution or regression is and is likely to remain the political.

The Soviet Union (and the States formed later on its model) has always been the most political of countries—and indeed prides itself on the fact. Its system is one in which a wider section of the citizen's life is considered to fall within the competence of the governing party than is often the case. At the same time, political instruction is continually given, and people at their places of work are often assembled to vote approval of some act of the State, or of foreign Communists. Yet this political activity is limited. The citizen is the object of more politics than with us, but practically speaking he is the initiator of none: he is always at the receiving end.

The theoretical justification for the one-party system is that on a Marxist view any party reflects the attitudes of a given class, defends its interests and provides its programme. Therefore, in the Soviet Union, where the anti-proletarian classes have long become extinct, there is no need for a second party. In fact, in Russia the opposition parties were suppressed when the classes they were presumed to represent were still very much in existence, so the argument is in any case very much an *ex post facto* justification. And even now it is only by a formal classification that the collectivised peasantry is taken

[7]

(for certain purposes only) as not constituting a class different from the proletariat.

Marx stood in general for political liberty. It is true that he spoke of the 'dictatorship' of the proletariat, but he also spoke of the British régime, under which he himself freely worked and organised and wrote, as a 'dictatorship' of the bourgeoisie. Freedom of the Press prevailed under the one régime he recognised as a dictatorship of the proletariat, the Paris Commune, even though its short career was one of permanent crisis and civil war. He took the party of the proletariat (coming to power, as he expected, in a country with a proletarian majority) to be the natural majority once the institutional and economic grip of the bourgeoisie had been broken. The opposition parties would, on this view, fade away as the classes they had represented ceased to exist.

It is recognised that in reality many more parties may exist in a State than there are classes. All types of Socialist, social-democrat, anarchist and syndicalist parties and groups are admitted to be 'working class'. At the time of the Revolution, the Mensheviks were not denied this title. It is true that the non-Communist proletarian parties are said to represent the influence among the proletariat of petit-bourgeois ideas. But if it comes to that there is now no Communist Party which has not recently been accused by another of the same fault.

When we turn to actual history, it is plain that by the early nineteen-twenties the Russian working class, which had always been somewhat ambiguous in its attitude to the new régime, had become thoroughly disenchanted. Menshevism gained ground—and was suppressed. 'Worker' factions in the Party itself proliferated in the factories—and were crushed. The great workers' movement which culminated in the Kronstadt Rebellion was put down in bloodshed. Finally, when Stalin came to power, the residual defence of working-class interests put up by moderate Bolsheviks was eliminated. The alleged 'representation' of the workers by the Communist Party of the Soviet Union is based on theory rather than on the freely ascertained views of the working class. But, as Engels remarked, 'The official programme of the Party is less important than what it actually does.'* It would probably be more realistic to regard the Communist Party as an autonomous organisa-

* Letter to Bebel, March 1875. Quoted in Appendix I, *Critique of the Gotha Programme*, London 1933.

[8]

tion of a type not foreseen by Marx, or even, if an economic rather than a political basis is deemed necessary, the representative of Djilas' New Class—the Soviet priviligentsia taken as a whole.

It is worth noting that the idea of combining political liberty with the Soviet system has exercised Communists who shared, or returned to, the view of Marx and Rosa Luxemburg that its absence was bound to lead to the degeneration of the State. Bukharin himself, while an old Communist and Marxist, hoped in 1936 for the legalisation of a second party, not indeed as a force opposed to the régime, but as a vehicle of 'changes and remedies'.* And, if not in this particular form, it is clear that the problem continues to exercise many thoughtful Communists, in Russia as elsewhere.

The USSR is the only country in the world whose very name is merely a description of its State system (as is its most common official abbreviation, 'the Soviet Union'). The key word is Soviet; one speaks of a Soviet achievement, or a Soviet citizen. Yet the word Soviet is no more than the Russian rendering of the English word 'Council'. To a Russian at the beginning of this century it would have conveyed no political, let alone territorial or patriotic, meaning. The original Soviets of Workers' Deputies sprang up in the 1905 Revolution as more or less spontaneous strike and insurrectionary committees (just as they have done in similar circumstances, such as the anti-Russian rising in Hungary in 1956). Lenin, who till then had not developed a particular view of the form of organisation suitable to the workers' movement and the workers' state, greeted them as the method he sought. Marx and Engels had regarded the democratic republic, as it had developed in the nineteenth century, as the correct form for the 'dictatorship of the proletariat'.

When the 1917 Revolution came, Soviets again formed both in the factories and in the Army. These action committees elected delegates to a central congress which first met in June. Meanwhile, the Petrograd Soviet formed a power not necessarily hostile to, but at least largely independent of, the new Provisional Government, and exerted almost as much practical power in the capital. The Bolsheviks were at first a minority in it, as in the other Soviets. It was only in the autumn that

* *Power and the Soviet Elite*, Boris A. Nicolaevsky, London 1965, pp. 15–16.

[9]

the Bolsheviks were able to gain a majority and, on November 7, to seize power not simply as a political group, but in the name of the Petrograd Soviet. The Second Congress of Soviets, meeting the same evening, was then declared the supreme State body, and a majority of it was induced to accept the *fait accompli* and confirm the new Bolshevik government. The new form of State rested, as no previous form had, on the factories. It is true that soon coercion, and the silencing of not only moderate Socialist but also moderate Communist trends, cast doubt on the genuine representativeness of the Soviets now elected in them. Nevertheless, in principle, and in form, this was an unprecedented type of state, and it was not out of place to describe it as such.

But, by a curious paradox, the Soviets based on the workers at their place of work ceased to exist in the thirties. Under the Soviet Constitution which came into force in 1936, the *form* of the State is hardly distinguishable from many countries in the West. The lower Soviets have become territorial units, like British town councils, and the Supreme Soviet is (in principle at least) elected simply through constituencies in the normal western Parliamentary manner. The word Soviet no longer has any specific meaning differentiating the USSR from other countries.

On the governmental and ministerial side, Lenin had spoken of 'destroying' rather than taking over the bourgeois State. and greatly blamed moderate Social Democrats for not sharing this view. But though after the Revolution the body nominating the government was theoretically the Congress of Soviets rather than Tsar, Duma or Constituent Assembly (and in practice was the Central Committee of the Communist Party), the State machinery which the ministers thus nominated took over was in fact the old Tsarist machine. Lenin recognised this, saying that all the Communists had done was to anoint the old Russian bureaucracy with Soviet holy oil.* In his time there were a number of attempts to set up bodies to control this bureaucracy. But he recognised that these in their turn became bureaucratised (for example, the Workers' and Peasants' Inspection—Rabkrin). As late as 1916 he had believed that it would be possible for workers to become governmental officials, or even members of the government, for a year or so, and then go back to the work bench. He underestimated (apart

* Lenin: Sochineniya. Vol. XXXVI, p. 559.

from anything else) the complexity of the modern State. In fact, far from this rather Utopian development, the bureaucracy became larger and larger, and more and more able to defend its positions, until in the end it had developed into a highly differentiated group.

The Constitution of 1936 was largely written by Bukharin (with some assistance from Karl Radek). Its author truly intended it to mark the return of the Soviet Union to a large measure of political and civil liberty. It is an almost impeccably liberal document, guaranteeing the personal rights of citizens, and their control of the state through free elections. 1936, the year which marked this apparently major shift towards liberalisation, was also the first year of the Great Purge, in which Stalin's personal dictatorship was established by unrestrained terror. At the same time, the forms of the Constitution were preserved: the first elections under the new style were held with much celebration while the single party destroyed within itself even that remnant of opposition represented by deviating or unenthusiastic Stalinists.

One article of the Constitution notably diverges from the normal liberal provisions—Article 126 which provides a special position for the Communist Party. This alone gives some hint of the realities. For there are, in effect, two political systems in the Soviet Union. That carrying out the will of the State is real, and full of life and power. That designed to give the impression that the citizen has in his turn a right to control the State lacks substance.

It has been said that the Party leadership in the Soviet Union aims to maintain its own power at all costs, and that the whole political machinery is designed either to perpetuate, or to conceal, this fact. And there is no doubt that elections at which only one candidate, selected with the approval of the Party, comes forward are not likely to provide much of the reality of democratic control by the voter. Nor would it be expected that a Supreme Soviet elected in this fashion would show much sign of being unamenable to the wishes of the Party leadership. All the same, the mere existence of these institutions, even in comparatively phantom form, is not without significance. If things change, they represent a legal and constitutional means already in existence, by which the popular will, and the various competing tendencies, might be expressed. There have been a number of occasions in history in

[11]

which institutions designed to do no more than make a good impression have unexpectedly come to life. For example, one may feel that Stalin intended the State independence of Poland or Hungary to be merely a respectable cover to his full power of control in these countries: nevertheless, when circumstances changed, this shadow independence was given a big measure of reality—which would not have been possible if they had been formally incorporated into the Soviet Union like Lithuania or Georgia.

Even now, prominent intellectuals appeal to the letter of the Constitution, and of the law. It is true that the Moscow students' demonstration on March 5, 1966, which carried the provocative banner 'Observe the Constitution' was broken up and its organisers sent to labour camps. Nevertheless, such demonstrations carry a certain meaning: the already existing Constitution is a programme for democracy. Moreover, it would perhaps be wrong to underestimate the difference between a dictatorship which presents itself as a 'democracy', and one which (like Hitler's) openly proclaims the anti-democratic principle. Under a Stalin, it is clear that there was no intention whatever of giving any practical effect to the libertarian documents of the state. But in less straightforward times the mere fact that the idea of democracy has persisted, even though distorted by doublethink, means that there is a reserve of aspiration in Communist minds as elsewhere.

Thus, in reading the factual material which follows on the formal and the real elements in Soviet politics, it may well be valuable to consider not only their past development and present structure, but also their future potentialities.

Acknowledgements are due to Messrs. L. Levine, H. S. Murray, and particularly M. Friedman, for their invaluable collaboration.

ROBERT CONQUEST

I

Development of the Constitution

On July 10, 1918, the Fifth All-Russian Congress of Soviets ratified the Constitution of the Russian Soviet Federative Socialist Republic. The structure of the State system as embodied in this Constitution represented a formal codification of institutions which already existed in fact. Since the Second All-Russian Congress of Soviets in November, 1917, the Congress had become the supreme organ of State power of the RSFSR. Under Article 25 of the new Constitution,[1] it was to consist of representatives of town Soviets on the basis of one deputy to 25,000 electors, and of representatives of *guberniya* (province) Congresses of Soviets on the basis of one deputy to 125,000 inhabitants. The disparity between the rights of the urban and rural populations in the election of deputies was obvious: the ratio of representation was considerably higher in the case of urban areas, while the rural deputies to the All-Russian Congress were, moreover, elected indirectly. This represented at once an assertion of the concept of proletarian leadership and a device to prevent the swamping of the Soviet machinery by the overwhelming numerical superiority of the peasantry.

In the six-monthly intervals between sessions of the Congress supreme power, *i.e.* legislative, administrative and controlling authority, was vested in the All-Russian Central Executive Committee (VTsIK) consisting of not more than 200 members elected by the Congress. The competence of the Congress and of the VTsIK was all-embracing; and, apart from the powers specifically listed in the Constitution, there was a further provision that they could decide all questions which they deemed to come within their jurisdiction. Only two powers were reserved exclusively to the Congress: (1) the establishing, supplementing and amendment of the basic principles of the Constitution of the RSFSR; and (2) the ratification of peace treaties. And, indeed, in practice it was not the Congress but its inner body, the VTsIK, which exercised the parliamentary function and continued to do so until 1936. It was, for instance, authorised to appoint the Council of People's Commissars and to direct the various branches of the Government and administration. Between sessions of the VTsIK (which, after the 7th Congress of Soviets in December, 1919, took place once in two months)[2] its Presidium was the highest legislative, administrative and controlling authority.

The tendency to transfer power from the representative to the executive body became progressively more pronounced throughout the whole system, in both Party and State, as the functions of the State became increasingly managerial. Even at this early stage it was not confined to the Congress of Soviets, whose unwieldy size made it more justifiable: it applied also to the local Soviets. The Petrograd Soviet of 1917, for instance, was from its inception largely managed and, for all practical purposes, replaced by its Executive Committee. And in March, 1919, the Eighth Party Congress passed a resolution deploring 'the tendency to refer the decision of all matters exclusively to the Executive Committees' of Soviets.[3]

The Constitution, which was also taken as the model for the Constitutions of the other Soviet Socialist Republics, provided at the same time for a hierarchical arrangement of local Soviets, extending downwards from the regional (*oblast*) level to the provincial (*guberniya*), county (*uyezd*), rural district (*volost*), town and village Soviets. Each level of local authority down to the rural district had its own Congress of Soviets and its own Executive Committee. Town and village Soviets also had their Executive Committees. The responsibilities of the local authorities were not, however, clearly defined. They were required to adopt 'all appropriate measures for developing the cultural and economic life of their territory' and to decide 'all questions of purely local importance'; but at the same time they were required to carry out 'all instructions issued by the appropriate higher organs of Soviet authority'.

The Constitution appeared to be designed to forestall a too literal interpretation of the slogan 'All power to the local Soviets', which had become widespread during the early phase of the revolution. Since the supreme State organs, the Congress and the VTsIK, were empowered to determine their own competence, the centralist trend in Soviet administration was apparent from the start. The local Soviets were essentially regarded as mere instruments of local administration, and their power of independent action was severely restricted. This was ensured most effectively by the Constitution's budgetary provisions. The budget estimates of local Soviets had to be approved by higher authority, and those of town, *guberniya* and *oblast* Soviets had to be ratified by the VTsIK and the Council of People's Commissars. In view of this, the description of the 1918 Constitution as 'federal' had little justification in fact.

The most obvious omission from the Constitution was any direct indication of where real power lay. Behind the façade of the Soviets was the Bolshevik Party which, despite the precarious survival of other Socialist parties, was already in virtual control of the Government apparatus and had arrogated to itself the right to speak as the sole voice of the people. This all-important fact of Party dictatorship was not reflected in the Fundamental Law of 1918 and was not given constitutional expression until 1936.

The doctrine of the separation of powers peculiar to Western democratic States was explicitly rejected by Lenin, who identified it with what he derisively called 'parliamentarism'. He condemned it as a subterfuge, designed to create an impression of popular rule and political freedom. It reduced parliaments to mere 'talking shops', while the real work of State was conducted behind the scenes by the non-representative executive branch.[4] The way out of 'parliamentarism', he said, quoting Marx, lay not in abolishing representative institutions and the elective system but in turning representative bodies into 'working' institutions. In his ten theses on the Soviet régime presented to the Seventh Party Congress in March, 1918, he recommended:[5]

'The abolition of parliamentarism (as the separation of legislative from executive work); the unifying of legislative and executive State work. The merging of administration and legislation.'

In this respect the provisions of the 1918 Constitution might be considered more in accordance with Marxist theory than was the subsequent Soviet practice of delimiting powers, although the theory has never been renounced. Legislative powers were not confined to the representative body, the Congress of Soviets, but were also shared by the VTsIK, the Presidium of the VTsIK, and the Council of People's Commissars. The charge levelled by the S.R.s and Mensheviks that the

Council of People's Commissars was arrogating the legislative rights of the VTsIK was countered by the argument that the rapid rate of development of events made it imperative for the Council of People's Commissars to be able to issue urgent decrees.[6] Decrees of the Council of People's Commissars of major political importance were to be submitted to the VTsIK, which had the right to annul them. In theory the Council was responsible to both the VTsIK and the Congress of Soviets, but it seems probable that its degree of accountability was largely determined by its own estimation of the urgency of the measures it proposed to enact. It is noticeable that the Soviet authorities, while condemning the alleged bourgeois practice of Government by decree, tend to minimise this immoderate strengthening of the executive branch of the Soviet Government—a feature which has by no means been eliminated despite the article in the 1936 Constitution which brought it to a formal close.

THE 1924 CONSTITUTION

The formation of the USSR, decided on at the end of 1922, necessitated a new Constitution. A drafting commission was set up by the Central Executive Committee (TsIK) of the USSR elected by the First Congress of Soviets of the USSR on January 10, 1923, and the first Constitution of the USSR was ratified by the Second Congress of Soviets of the USSR on January 31, 1924.

The Constitution established the Congress of Soviets of the USSR as the supreme organ of authority. Following the 1918 pattern, its membership consisted of representatives of urban Soviets on the basis of one deputy for every 25,000 voters, and representatives of *guberniya* (and later of *krai* and *oblast*) congresses of Soviets on the basis of one deputy for every 125,000. The Congress was convened annually for regular sessions, though from the time of the Fourth Congress of Soviets of the USSR (April, 1927) it was convened only once every two years.[7]

A special feature of the new Constitution was the changed structure of the TsIK. It now became a bicameral organ, consisting of a Union Council, designed to represent the general interests of all nationalities of the USSR, and a Council of Nationalities, whose function was to represent the specific interests of the various nationalities. The Union Council was elected by the Congress of Soviets on a proportional basis from representatives of the Union republics. The Council of Nationalities consisted of five representatives from each Union or autonomous republic and one representative from each autonomous *oblast*. They were elected by the Congresses of Soviets of the Union and Autonomous Republics and autonomous *oblasts* and were confirmed as members of the TsIK by the Congress of Soviets of the USSR.

The two chambers of the TsIK were unequal in numbers but had equal rights. Only agreed decisions of both chambers gave the force of law to decrees and regulations submitted to them. In the event of disagreement Conciliation Commissions were to be set up by the chambers on a parity basis to put forward a draft agreed decision. If agreement was still not reached the matter at issue could be referred to the Congress of Soviets at the request of one of the chambers. In the event, disagreement occurred only once during the life of the 1924 Constitution; at the Second Session of the TsIK of the USSR of the Second Convocation a draft decision put forward by a Conciliation Commission was accepted by both chambers.[8]

Each chamber of the TsIK elected its own Presidium of nine members, which arranged the agenda for its sittings and dealt with current matters between sessions. The Presidium of the TsIK itself, which was the supreme legislative, executive and administrative organ of power of the USSR in the period between sessions of the TsIK, consisted of the presidia of the two chambers plus nine other members elected at a joint session of the two chambers. The number of chairmen of the TsIK corresponded to the number of Union Republics and they also formed part of its Presidium.[9]

The TsIK of the USSR formed the Council of People's Commissars, consisting of a Chairman, Deputy Chairman, Chairman of the Supreme Council of National Economy and People's Commissars. It had the power to annul decrees of the Congresses of Soviets and the TsIKs of the Union Republics and of all other organs of State power throughout the territory of the USSR.

As under the 1918 Constitution, legislative power was exercised by both the representative and executive branches of government: the Congress of Soviets of the USSR, the TsIK of the USSR, the Presidium of the TsIK of the USSR, and the Council of People's Commissars of the USSR. The last-named was empowered to issue, within the limits of the rights granted to it, decrees and instructions whose execution was obligatory throughout the USSR. These could be annulled or suspended by the TsIK of the USSR and its Presidium.

The Constitution provided the pattern for the Constitutions of the Union and autonomous Republics, and their supreme organs of power had a similar structure. They had Republic Congresses of Soviets, Central Executive Committees (single chamber) with their presidia, and Republic Councils of People's Commissars.

The centralist trend apparent in the 1918 Constitution was intensified. The powers of the supreme organs of the USSR were enumerated in an all-embracing list, which left little scope to the initiative of the Union Republics. Three categories of People's Commissariats were established. The first category, of All-Union Commissariats which existed only in the Council of People's Commissars of the USSR, included Foreign Affairs, Military and Naval Affairs, Foreign Trade, Ways of Communication and Posts and Telegraphs. The second category, of unified (Union-Republican) commissariats, existed both in the Government of the USSR and in the Governments of the Union Republics, with the latter responsible for executing decisions taken at the centre.

This category included the Supreme Council of National Economy and the Commissariats of Food, Labour, Finance and of the Workers' and Peasants' Inspectorate. The third category, of 'Republic Commissariats', embraced Agriculture, Internal Affairs, Justice, Health, Education and Social Security. Most of these matters are ordinarily considered to be of local significance, but the central Government reserved the right to issue basic regulations covering all these fields. By 1936 only the last two of this list remained under Republican control: in 1929 agriculture was put under a unified Commissariat; in 1934 Internal Affairs, with the unified State Political Administration (OGPU), were brought under an All-Union Commissariat (in 1936 it became a Union-Republican Commissariat), and in 1936 Union-Republican Commissariats were formed to administer Justice and Health.

The trend towards centralisation was further reinforced by the programme of industrialisation inaugurated in the late twenties. The new industrial Commissariats were formed either on an All-Union or on a unified basis, with the Union Republics retaining authority only in the field of small-scale local industry. The fictitious nature of Soviet federalism was becoming increasingly apparent.

While existing arrangements provided a measure of decentralised administration for various government functions, policy remained under rigidly centralised control. For the policy of the USSR was determined by a single disciplined Party, the unified structure of which made nonsense of the façade of a federal State system and pseudo-representative Soviet institutions. The Soviets were defined in ideological terms as the 'State form of the dictatorship of the proletariat',[10] the 'most democratic of all possible State organisations while classes continue to exist. ... The power of the majority of the population over the minority'.[11]

In view of the electoral discrimination of the 1918 and 1924 Constitutions in favour of the proletarian minority, this last description is, to say the least, highly debatable. Nevertheless, there might have been an element of truth in the epithet 'democratic' if the Soviets themselves had been the initiators of State policy. But they had, in the eyes of the ruling Party, no independent *raison d'être*: they were merely a useful vehicle for the policy of a minority organisation, the Bolshevik Party. 'It is not,' said Stalin, 'merely a matter of the Soviets as such, but primarily a matter of who is to lead them'.[12] His own definition of their function qualified them as 'levers' or 'transmission belts' connecting the 'millions of working people with the vanguard of the proletariat'[13] (*i.e.*, the Party), while a Party resolution of 1930 described them as 'conductors of the general line of the Party'.[14]

But neither the Party's monopoly of power nor even its very existence was acknowledged by the 1924 Constitution. The moral justification of the Party's pre-eminent position rested on the entirely untested premise that the 'broad masses of non-Party workers regard our Party as *their* Party, as a Party *near* and *dear* to them, in whose expansion and consolidation they are vitally interested, and to whose leadership they voluntarily entrust their destiny.'[15]

THE 1936 CONSTITUTION

On February 1, 1935, a Plenum of the Party Central Committee instructed Molotov to appear before the Seventh Congress of Soviets of the USSR and propose changes in the Constitution directed towards:

(a) 'further democratising the electoral system by replacing not entirely equal suffrage by equal suffrage, indirect elections by direct elections, and the open ballot by the secret ballot', and
(b) 'giving more precise definition to the social and economic basis of the Constitution by bringing the Constitution into conformity with the present relation of class forces in the USSR (the creation of a new Socialist industry, the elimination of the *Kulak* class, the victory of the collective farm system, the consolidation of Socialist property on the basis of Soviet society, and so on)'.[16]

Molotov's motion was unanimously approved by the Congress of Soviets on February 6, and the TsIK appointed a Commission under Stalin's chairmanship to draft the text of a new Constitution. On June 1, 1936, Stalin submitted a draft to a Central Committee plenum which approved it and ordered the convocation of an extraordinary session of the Congress of Soviets to ratify it. Meanwhile, the text of the draft was released for public discussion. There are said to have been 154,000 amendments suggested by organisations and individuals; of these only 43 were accepted, and only one, the substitution of direct for indirect election of the Council of Nationalities, was of more than verbal significance.[17]

On November 25, 1936, Stalin presented the final draft of the new Constitution to the Extraordinary Eighth All-Union Congress of Soviets, which approved it unanimously on December 5.

A clue to the motives behind the drafting of a new Constitution was provided by Stalin's report to the Extraordinary Eighth Congress of Soviets. He contended that a Constitution, as distinct from a programme of future aims, should be the 'registration and legislative embodiment of what has already been achieved and won in fact.' The new Constitution was required to reflect and record that changes had occurred since 1924 in the country's economic and social structure. Stalin proclaimed the complete victory of Socialism in the national economy and outlined the social metamorphosis which was its consequence.

With the elimination of exploitation the working class could no longer be called a proletariat. Its dictatorship had entered its second stage, that of Socialism, which he also rather confusingly described as the first stage of Communism. Landlords,

Kulaks and capitalists had been eliminated, and there remained only two friendly classes, the workers and peasants, whose interests were no longer in conflict. The intelligentsia, the only other specific social group, were not a class but a stratum, 80 or 90 per cent of whose members came from the working class and peasantry. For this reason it was possible to introduce universal suffrage with no disenfranchised classes and to abolish the inequality between workers and peasants as expressed in indirect elections and the weighting of the votes in favour of urban workers rather than in that of the peasants. Stalin claimed that all classes were now loyal to the régime and that elections could become secret. At the same time, he attempted to justify the preservation of the Communist Party's monopoly position and the denial of freedom to other parties by the casuistic premise that political parties merely represent 'antagonistic classes': in the absence of the latter, the need for more than a single party did not arise.

The Communist Party defended the interests of the working masses and provided 'democracy for the working people', that is, in terms of his own definition of the existing class structure, for all. 'That is why', he declared, 'I think that the Constitution of the USSR is the only thoroughly democratic Constitution in the world.'[18]

In the post-Stalin period it was, however, admitted that: 'Many of the democratic forms of life provided for by the USSR Constitution of 1936 did not at the time find proper development and were distorted.'[19]

The reassertion of the Party's position as the ruling group meant that the régime, in its main essentials, remained unchanged. Stalin's motive for announcing with such elaborate ceremony what were really incidental changes was to be found not so much in consideration of internal policy as in international circumstances. 'The international significance of the new Constitution', he said, 'can hardly be exaggerated.'[20] The threat to the Soviet Union implicit in Hitler's rise to power made it expedient to give some assurance of reliability to potential allies and to help to foster the idea of popular fronts by pacifying liberal opinion abroad. This same motive—the desire to demonstrate that the Soviet régime was moving in a democratic direction and enjoyed the full support of the Soviet people—explains the entirely unprecedented step of throwing a legislative proposal open to public discussion. For, though

[21]

its effect in terms of substantive changes in the text of the new Constitution was negligible, the discussion helped to create at any rate an appearance, both at home and abroad, of wide public support for the Soviet leaders and the régime they represented.

Although it has been amended in some details since it was first promulgated, the 1936 Constitution of the USSR remains in effect today. It consists of 13 chapters: (i) The Social Structure; (ii) The State Structure; (iii) The Higher Organs of State Power in the USSR; (iv) The Higher Organs of State Power in the Union Republics; (v) The Organs of State Administration of the USSR; (vi) The Organs of State Administration of the Union Republics; (vii) The Higher Organs of State Power in the Autonomous Soviet Socialist Republics; (viii) The Local Organs of State Power; (ix) The Courts and the Procurator's Office; (x) Fundamental Rights and Duties of Citizens; (xi) The Electoral System; (xii) Arms, Flag, Capital; (xiii) Procedure for Amending the Constitution.

The differentiation between 'organs of State power' and 'organs of State administration' draws a line between elected organs and those established by appointment. The former are the Soviets at all levels, and their presidia and executive committees; the latter embrace the Ministries and the Councils of Ministers of the USSR, the Union Republics and the autonomous Republics. As has already been indicated, this distinction would appear to represent a departure from the early Marxist concept of the Commune State in which the people would be actively involved in both legislation and administration. The 'local organs of power' referred to in Chapter VIII are the Soviets of territorial areas from *krai* and *oblast* downwards, *i.e.* those Soviets which are not qualified as 'supreme'.

A number of the articles of Chapters I and X of the Constitution are virtually meaningless, inasmuch as no provision is made to guarantee the rights they purport to confer. Article 7 in Chapter I, for instance, states that 'every household in a collective farm . . . has . . . as its personal property, a subsidiary husbandry, a dwelling-house, livestock, poultry, and minor agricultural implements . . .' But this is merely an affirmation of what is permitted: none of the items specified is provided by the State.

Similarly, Article 125, in Chapter X, which purports to guarantee the basic civil freedoms, states that 'these civil rights are ensured by placing at the disposal of the working people and their organisations printing presses, stocks of paper, public buildings, the streets, communications facilities, and other material requisites for the exercise of these rights'. Yet the State does not make free provision of printing presses and stocks of paper. The article is really no more than an assertion of the State's control over these facilities, and a reminder that only approved organisations may engage, within prescribed limits, in the printing and circulation of information.

There are still other rights whose interpretation is less ambiguous but which also lack provision for their enforcement. Article 127, for example, provides that 'citizens of the USSR are guaranteed inviolability of the person. No person may be placed under arrest except by decision of a Court or with the sanction of a procurator.' But the frequency and the ease with which this fundamental right has been flouted was attested to by Khrushchev in his 1956 'secret' speech.[21] In view of this, there is irony in Stalin's assertion that the Constitution 'does not confine itself to stating the formal rights of citizens but especially stresses the guarantees of those rights'.[22]

Chapter X contains one very important article, Article 126, which, in stating the rights of Soviet citizens to unite in public organisations and societies, adds that the 'most active and politically conscious citizens ... voluntarily unite in the Communist Party of the Soviet Union, which is the vanguard of the working people in their struggle to build a Communist society and is the leading core of all organisations of the working people, both public and State'.

This is the first mention of the Communist Party in a Russian or Soviet Constitution, and, although it appears in an otherwise insignificant article, it is the most far-reaching statement of all. It nullifies the democratic pretensions of a large section of the Constitution by its clear indication that policy leadership is concentrated in a minority organisation which is not open to all citizens but embraces only those arbitrarily described as the 'most active and politically-conscious'.

Chapter II deals with the rights of the Union Republics: to have their own Constitutions, which take 'account of the specific features of the Republic' and are 'drawn up in full conformity with the Constitution of the USSR' (Article 16); 'freely to secede from the USSR' (Article 17); to enter into direct relations with foreign States and to conclude agreements and exchange diplomatic and consular representatives with them' (Article 18a), and to have their own military formations (18b).

Article 15 states that the sovereignty of the Union Republics is limited only by the federal powers enumerated in Article 14. But these are defined in very comprehensive terms which leave extremely little to the initiative of the Republics, and include even the right to determine the basic principles in a number of spheres primarily of local interest (*e.g.* education and justice) for which the Federal Government may not be departmentally responsible.

Certain rights formally granted to the Union Republics were clearly never intended to become operative; or at least the likelihood of their being invoked was considered negligible. At least one official Soviet source has stated that this was the case with the provisions of Article 17—the right to secession.[23] Stalin's motive in not accepting a proposed amendment to delete the article from the Constitution no doubt derived partly from its potential propaganda value abroad[24] and probably also from reluctance to depart officially from Leninist doctrine. Articles 18a (right of diplomatic representation) and 18b (right to their own military formations) have also been more honoured in the breach. A measure of the importance attached to the first is the fact that, as far as can be ascertained, Lithuania has no Foreign Minister (none was included in the government formed after the last 1963 election) while the Latvian Foreign Minister's duties are not so onerous as to prevent his being simultaneously Minister of Education. Those Republics which maintain Foreign Ministries, including the Ukraine and Byelorussia, which by virtue of their 'independence' have their own seats in UNO, have all consistently declined offers from foreign Powers to establish direct diplomatic relations.

Article 18b appears to be a dead letter since no Republic maintains a Defence Ministry or its own armed forces.

On the question of legislation the Constitution is studiously uninformative. Thus, while Article 32 states that 'legislative power in the USSR is exercised exclusively by the Supreme Soviet of the USSR', the Presidium of the Supreme Soviet of the USSR and the Council of Ministers enact provisions tantamount to legislation.[25] The Supreme Soviet itself meets normally only twice a year and its sessions last only a few days.

The bulk of current legislation is enacted in between

sessions by the Presidium, which issues edicts in continuance of the practice established under the 1924 Constitution; and part of the time of the normal Supreme Soviet session is usually taken up by formal ratification of legislation already operative.

The abolition or re-establishment of Ministries over the years has probably been the subject of more *ex post facto* legislation than anything else. The ninth session of the Supreme Soviet of the fourth convocation held in December, 1957, for example, confirmed edicts of the Supreme Soviet Presidium issued in May (only 20 days after the previous Supreme Soviet session), July, August and December of that year, amalgamating, re-designating, instituting or abolishing whole series of Ministries and Committees of the Council of Ministers; and this involved deletions and insertions in three articles of Chapter V of the Constitution.

In the past there has often been a much longer interval between promulgation of edicts by the Presidium and decrees of the Council of Ministers and their confirmation as laws by the Supreme Soviet. In 1940 a tuition fee was enacted (by decree of the Council of Peoples' Commissars) for the higher classes of secondary schools and for higher education, contrary to Article 121, which then stated that education was free to all; on June 26 of the same year, although Article 119 proclaimed a seven-hour working day, an edict of the Presidium extended it to eight hours; in February, 1944, foreign affairs and defence were added to the powers of the Union Republics; in July, 1944, determination of the principles of legislation on marriage and the family was added to the federal power; and in October, 1945, the lower age-limit for deputies to the Supreme Soviet was raised to 23.

Only in February, 1947, were these changes, already operative, reconciled with the Constitution by amendment of the relevant articles.

It would appear, therefore, that the Presidium, in practice, continues to exercise the full power of the Supreme Soviet between sessions, although the 1936 Constitution delegates to the Presidium in these circumstances only the power of appointment and dismissal of Ministers and the power to declare war. This divergence of theory from practice—a recurrent feature in Soviet government—exposes the hollowness of Stalin's claim (again, no doubt intended for foreign audiences) to reserve the power of legislation exclusively to the representative body. In his report to the Extraordinary Eighth All-Union Congress of Soviets, he demonstratively rejected a proposed amendment to the Constitution which would have given the Presidium power to make provisional legislative enactments.[26] Nevertheless, it continues to exercise this power in practice, and a Soviet legal authority has recently condemned this anomaly.[27]

Stalin's own definition of the Constitution, however, as the legislative embodiment of what has been achieved in practice as distinct from a programme of plans for the future, provides a form of theoretical loop-hole for the practice of *ex post facto* amendments. The implication of the definition is that if practice or expediency are at variance with the Constitution it may be the latter which requires modification, inasmuch as it has ceased to be a faithful record of the *de facto* position.

There is a striking contrast between the unceremonious manner in which the Constitution has been changed in practice and the formal provisions of the Constitution which require for its amendment a majority of not less than two-thirds of the votes in each chamber of the Supreme Soviet. Since there is no record of any vote in the Supreme Soviet being less than unanimous, the ratification of amendments to the Constitution has become an empty formality.

Striking proof of this was given by the publication in 1953 of an amended version of the Constitution containing 'changes and additions adopted at the First, Second, Third, Fourth and Fifth sessions of the Supreme Soviet of the Third Convocation'. The details of publication which, according to Soviet censorship law, must be appended to every printed work, reveal that the amended text was set up for printing on June 17 and that permission to begin printing was given on July 11—four weeks before an amendment to Article 126 was ratified at the fifth session, which opened on August 5, 1953. The likelihood of the amendment's not being approved was evidently considered so remote that 300,000 copies of the amended Constitution were printed.

It is clear that the Constitution is not a reliable guide to the current organisation of the Soviet system of government. Since, in any case, relatively few of the rules and orders which govern the lives of Soviet citizens are in the form of formal law, the latter needs to be supplemented by general legislation if one is to obtain a picture of how the system works. Unfortunately this source, too, is defective. The legislation published in the official journal of the USSR Supreme Soviet[28] is defective in detail, while the enactments of the Council of Ministers,[29] which constitute the major body of current legislation, have not been regularly available since 1949.

An article in the official Government newspaper at the end of 1956[30] complained of the non-publication of Government decrees and regulations, and pointed out the practical difficulties arising. Knowledge of Soviet law was the main guarantee in strengthening Socialist legality, the paper said, but, unfortunately,

'this is sometimes impossible because some decrees and instructions of the Government, by no means of a secret nature, are sent to institutions and enterprises but remain unknown not only to the broad category of citizens but even to individuals who must know them, for example, legal counsel to enterprises, jurists working in legal aid offices and practising lawyers'.

This unsatisfactory state of affairs is partially recognised by an edict of the Presidium of the USSR Supreme Soviet of June 19, 1958, on procedure for the publication and entry into force of acts of the Supreme Soviet and its Presidium.[31] This, unfortunately, does not cover the more important legislation of the Council of Ministers, but the edict instructs the Council to establish a procedure for the publication and entry into force of its own enactments. It establishes that laws of the USSR, decrees and other acts of the USSR Supreme Soviet, and edicts and decrees of its Presidium, should be published in *Vedomosti Verkhovnogo Soveta SSSR* in the languages of the Union Republics not later than seven days after adoption. The more important and urgent of these should be published in *Izvestiya Sovetov Deputatov Trudyashchikhsya SSSR*, the official Government newspaper, and, if necessary, transmitted by radio and telegraph. Certain edicts and decrees of the Presidium not of general significance or of a normative character are to be circulated to the particular institutions and departments they concern, with the Presidium reserving the right, however, to decide whether or not they should be published. Some of the instructions of the 1958 decree were not enforced for very long. The practice of publishing laws in minority languages was abandoned after April, 1960. A decree of September 3, 1965, ordered once more that this be done.

While the Constitution refers to the various administrative orders and instructions which the executive is empowered to issue, it makes no mention of the machinery of the Party or the measures the Party enacts either alone or in conjunction with one or more of the State organs. Nevertheless, these con- stitute perhaps the most important legislative measures of all inasmuch as they are usually directives determining the prin- ciples of policy, both domestic and external. Such measures frequently remain unpublished or become known long after their enactment—even when they are enacted jointly with a State organ. For example, a Decree of the Central Committee of the CPSU and the Council of Ministers of the USSR, dated September 15, 1956, concerned with the organisation of boarding-schools was not published at the time, and its exist- ence became known only a year or more later when it was included in a volume of selected Party and Government legis- lative documents primarily intended as a handbook for officials in the Party apparatus.[32]

There are also instances of newly-enacted laws, especially juridical laws, being referred to orally by persons of authority, but not being printed in any publication. In other instances, an act is not printed in the special publications which exist for that purpose, but appears considerably later in an anno- tated edition of the Civil or Criminal Codex.[33] It is thus vir- tually impossible to discover what the law is at any given moment. The official no doubt has the guidance and help of departmental instructions, many of which can be presumed to be confidential. Some officials, but not all, will also be per- mitted to see the Party directives, open or restricted, on which policy is based. But such selectivity and differentiation in the routeing of information must make uniformity of practice very difficult, and must also lead to innumerable inquiries, through official or private channels, as to what the official line is on particular issues. The public, in particular, must on occasions be very much in the dark as to how they stand with the authorities.

The Constitution itself offers little practical help and it is unlikely that it is often consulted by administrators. The real Constitution, in the sense of a guide to the practical working of the body politic, does not exist as an open document but consists largely in understandings between individuals and in information whose circulation is restricted in one degree or another.

The need for a new Constitution, which would 'reflect the

vast changes that have taken place in the life of Soviet society',[34] was referred to at the 21st (1959) and 22nd (1961) Party Congresses, and in April, 1962, a constitutional commission, presided over by Khrushchev, was established. Brezhnev succeeded Khrushchev in this post after the latter's overthrow in October, 1964. So far the commission has not produced a draft.

The value of the written constitutional documents of the USSR is less of a practical than a symbolic and propaganda character. Their value in terms of external propaganda has already been mentioned; their internal propaganda value lies in the impression they create, in theory at least, of a settled order, consistent government, and inalienable civil rights. And for the Union and autonomous republics their own Constitutions exist, if not as guarantees, at any rate as gratifying symbols of theoretical sovereignty or statehood.

SOURCES

1. Lipatov and Savenkov, p. 147.
2. B.S.E., 1st edn., Vol. 13, p. 651.
3. KPSS v Rezolyutsiakh, Part 1, p. 445.
4. Lenin, Sochineniya, Vol. 25, p. 395.
5. Ibid., Vol. 27, p. 129.
6. Askerov et al., p. 378.
7. Denisov, p. 8.
8. Askerov et al., p. 340 (Note).
9. Ibid.
10. Stalin; Problems of Leninism, p. 54.
11. Ibid., p. 56.
12. Ibid., p. 552.
13. Ibid., p. 166.
14. KPSS v Rezolyutsiakh, Part II, p. 633.
15. Stalin; Problems of Leninism, p. 99.
16. Ibid., p. 679.
17. Ibid., p. 679ff.
18. Ibid.
19. Sovetskoe Gosudarstvo i Pravo, No. 10, 1962 (article by F. M. Burlatsky).
20. Stalin; Problems of Leninism, p. 679 ff.
21. The Dethronement of Stalin, pp. 14, 17.
22. Stalin; Problems of Leninism, p. 692.
23. Askerov et al., p. 254.
24. Stalin; Problems of Leninism, p. 704.
25. Gsovski, Vol. 1, p. 223.
26. Stalin; Problems of Leninism, p. 708.
27. Sovetskoe Gosudarstvo i Pravo, No. 12, 1966, p. 27.
28. Vedomosti Verkhovnogo Soveta SSSR.
29. Sobraniye Postanovlenii i Rasporyazhenii Soveta Ministrov SSSR.
30. Izvestiya, December 2, 1956.
31. Vedomosti Verkhovnogo Soveta SSSR, No. 14, 1958.
32. V. N. Malin et al., p. 289.
33. The New Leader, May 5, 1958 (article by Gsovski).
34. Pravda, December 6, 1962.

II

The Territorial—Administrative Structure

The Union of Soviet Socialist Republics is a federal State of 15 constituent republics called Union Republics. The Union Republic (or Soviet Socialist Republic) constitutes the highest form of statehood in the USSR and is formally a sovereign State with the right of secession. The conditions necessary for a given territory to achieve Union Republic status were set forth by Stalin at the Extraordinary Eighth All-Union Congress of Soviets on November 25, 1936. At the present time the USSR consists of the following constituent republics: the Russian Soviet Federative Socialist Republic (RSFSR) and the Ukrainian, Byelorussian, Uzbek, Kazakh, Georgian, Azerbaidzhan, Lithuanian, Moldavian, Latvian, Kirghiz, Tadzhik, Armenian, Turkmen and Estonian Soviet Socialist Republics (SSR).

The criterion of the suitability of an area to be established as an autonomous unit is that of nationality and this, in practice, has become identified with language. There are a number of national minority groups whose 'autonomy' derives simply from the fact of their having their own written language. In the early days of the USSR the central authorities, in reaction to the 'Russification' associated with Tsardom, showed great readiness to recognise distinctive language groups and to grant them autonomous status. Such groups, whose 'autonomy' has in certain cases survived the numerical decline of the peoples concerned into a minority inside the area to which they give their names (*e.g.* Bashkiria), are the so-called autonomous republics (ASSR), autonomous *oblasts* and national *okrugs*. The majority of the autonomous republics and *oblasts* and all the national *okrugs* are in the RSFSR. The autonomous republics in the RSFSR are the Bashkir, Buryat-Mongolian, Dagestan, Kabardino-Balker, Kalmyk, Karelian, Komi, Mari, Mordovian,

North-Ossetian, Tatar, Tuva, Udmurt, Chechen-Ingush, Chuvash and Yakut ASSRSs. In Azerbaidzhan there is the Nakhichevan, in Georgia the Abkhazian and Adzharian, and in Uzbekistan the Kara-Kalpak ASSRs.

The RSFSR contains the Adygei, Gorno-Altai, Jewish, Karachai-Cherkess, and Khakass autonomous *oblasts*. In Azerbaidzhan there is the Nagorno-Karabakh, in Georgia the South-Ossetian, and in Tadzhikistan the Gorno-Badakhshan autonomous *oblasts*. There are ten national *okrugs*, all in the RSFSR.

No autonomous or national unit is contained in another; they are all directly subordinate to the relevant Union Republic or administrative subdivision. Autonomous status confers no obvious political advantage over the administrative type of territorial division: the autonomous *oblast* differs from the administrative *oblast* only in the use of its national language for official business, while autonomous republics differ from autonomous *oblasts* and national *okrugs* only in having the titular forms of republics—Constitutions, Supreme Soviets (since 1936), ministers and Supreme Courts. Like *oblasts*, however, they are directly subordinate to the Union Republics.

Apart from the territorial units based on nationality and token autonomy, there are others, far more numerous, based purely on considerations of economic administration. Consequently, their structure is extremely fluid and may change as economic expediency dictates. Until February, 1957, when changes in *oblast* divisions became a Union Republic responsibility, such changes involved very frequent amendments to Articles 22, 23, 26, 27, 28, 29 and 29b of the USSR Constitution. It is now the Constitutions of those Union Republics which have an *oblast* division that will require repeated amendment. For example, on April 23, 1957, the Arzamas *oblast* of the RSFSR, which on March 3 had elected its *oblast* Soviet, was abolished and its territory incorporated into the Gorky *oblast*.[1]

The administrative-territorial units in descending order of size and importance are the *krai* (territory) *oblast* (region), *raion* (district), town, village (or rural locality) and urban-type settlement, which may be classified as a workers' settlement (*rabochi poselok*), health resort (*kurortny poselok*) or a residential summer resort (*dachni poselok*). Apart from the *krai* the highest administrative-territorial unit is the *oblast*, which is supposed

[31]

to be a unit of complex economic character containing both manufacturing industry and agriculture.[2] The *krais*, of which there are six, all in the RSFSR, are of *oblast* status but usually also contain an autonomous *oblast*. The only exception is the *Primorski* (Maritime) *Krai*, which probably owes its designation to its formation in 1938 by the division of the former Far Eastern *krai*, the rest of which became a *krai* of the normal type.

Six of the 15 Union Republics are divided into administrative *oblasts*. These are the RSFSR, the Ukrainian SSR, the Byelorussian SSR, the Uzbek SSR, the Kazakh SSR and the Kirghiz SSR. The remaining Union Republics are divided, like the *krais* and *oblasts*, into *raions*. 'The *raion* is organised in such a way as to take account of the need to provide guidance on Socialist large-scale agriculture and the local industry connected with it. It is the main link, the nodal point, of Socialist construction in the countryside.'[3] This refers to the so-called rural *raions*. Certain major towns of over 100,000 population are also sub-divided into *raions*. In each Union Republic the biggest towns are regarded as individual administrative units in their own right and are directly subordinate to the Republican administrative organs. Other towns, depending on their size and population, may be administratively subordinate either to the *oblast* or to the *raion*.

Villages or, more accurately, rural localities, are usually referred to administratively in terms of 'village soviets' (*Selsovety*), since a single village soviet may administer several scattered villages in a given area.

At the lower end of the administrative-territorial scale are the settlements (*poselki*), which have grown up in certain localities, often around industrial enterprises. Their development varies: some become absorbed into existing towns; others develop independently and achieve the status of towns. The progressive urbanisation of the country can be seen in the frequent announcements of such development and in the advancement of towns from *raion* subordination to *oblast* or Republic subordination.

THE SOVIET STRUCTURE

The Soviet State administrative system consists of a pyramidal hierarchy of soviets covering the whole country. The central and leading bodies of this apparatus are the USSR Supreme Soviet, the Presidium of the USSR Supreme Soviet and the USSR Council of Ministers. These bodies have their republican counterparts in the Union and autonomous republics; and within these republics the State system is completed by the local soviets, which carry on the administration at the various territorial levels, *i.e.* the *krai, oblast, okrug, raion,* city and village soviets. The Constitutions of the Union republics also mention two other links; the settlement soviets and the city *raion* soviets in those large cities which have *raion* subdivision.

The USSR State system is a unitary structure in which the administrative units participate not with particular rights and different interests but in accordance with a strictly graduated scale of subordination. As one Soviet author has put it,

'Local soviets do not, naturally, possess the right of deciding general State issues; such issues come within the competence of the higher organs of State power and State administration. On the other hand, neither is the competence of the individual links of the system of local soviets the same: the higher local soviets possess wider competence compared with the lower ones; the scale of their activity and the compass of the matters they can decide are wider than those of the lower soviets; the lower soviets are under the control of, and accountable to, the higher ones and work under their direction. A higher soviet is empowered to annul the enactments of lower soviets.'[4]

The basic organisational principle of both the Communist Party and of the State administrative apparatus is said to be 'democratic centralism'. This is contrasted with the so-called 'bureaucratic centralism' attributed to bourgeois societies, in which, allegedly, orders are passed down from the centre without the preliminary sounding of opinion below. In its application to the State apparatus 'democratic centralism' is officially defined in the following terms:

'(a) all organs of State power at the centre and in the localities are elected by the people;
(b) deputies are accountable to the electors;
(c) electors are granted the right to recall deputies;
(d) the leading organs of State administration are formed by the representative organs: at the centre, the Councils of Ministers by the Supreme Soviets; in the localities, the executive committees by the local Soviets;

(e) all organs of State power and organs of State administration form a single system, based on the strictest subordination of lower organs to the direction and control of higher organs;

(f) enactments of higher organs are binding on lower organs.'[5]

Superficially, these provisions appear to bear a democratic character. But, in practice, it is the two final clauses of the definition that are of primary significance. It is their application which ensures the 'strict unity and coordination of the actions of all the parts of the State machinery throughout the territory of the USSR.'[6]

Another feature of 'democratic centralism' as applied to the State apparatus is the principle of 'dual subordination', *i.e.*, the simultaneous subordination of a State organ to two higher organs. This means that departments of lower soviets are responsible both to the soviet's executive committee (*Ispolkom*), and so to the soviet at the level at which they work, and also to the corresponding department in their own line of business at the next higher level, up to the relevant Ministry. For example, the finance department of a *raion* soviet is subordinate, horizontally, to the executive committee of the *raion* soviet and, vertically, to the finance department of the next higher, *i.e.*, the *oblast*, soviet.[7] In practice, it is the 'vertical' line of command, leading up towards the centre, which has proved more effective than the 'horizontal' line of control by local soviets. The result is a tightly centralized administrative State, which at the same time preserves the useful propaganda myth of mass political activity through the medium of the local soviets. It should be noted that the principle of dual subordination applies only to locally elected bodies, *i.e.*, the soviets and their departments. It is explicitly stated that it does not apply to the local organs of the KGB, Ministry of Defence, Procuratura and other bodies, 'in the organisation and activity of which strict centralisation is necessary'.[8]

SOURCES

1. *Vedomosti Verkhovnogo Soveta SSSR*, No. 10, 1957.
2. Askerov *et. al.*, pp. 268–9.
3. *Ibid.*, p. 269.
4. Luzhin, *Gorodskie Sovety Deputatov Trudyashchikhsya*, p. 19.
5. *B.S.E.*, 2nd edn., Vol. 13, p. 656.
6. *Ibid.*
7. *Ibid.*, p. 479.
8. *Ibid.*, Chkhikvadze, pp. 96, 386.

III

The Electoral System

Under the 1918 and 1924 Constitutions electoral rights were granted and electoral procedure arranged for the primary purpose of reinforcing an avowed class dictatorship. The nature of the electoral law was largely determined by the fact that during this period elections were held in areas, especially rural areas, which were not dominated by the Bolsheviks. The main popular support for the Bolsheviks lay in the towns and workers' settlements, and for this reason the voting system was weighted heavily in favour of the urban proletariat. Before 1936 only the lowest level of soviets (*i.e.* the village, settlement, town and town-*raion* soviets) were elected directly. At higher levels there were Congresses of Soviets, extending through the various territorial stages to federal level. The town soviets elected delegates directly to all the Congresses of Soviets (*uyezd* or *raion, okrug, guberniya, krai* or *oblast*, Union Republic and All-Union); in the case of delegates representing rural areas, however, a multi-stage system operated whereby they were elected to a particular Congress of Soviets by the congress immediately lower in the hierarchy. Moreover, the norms of representation favoured the urban workers: the apportionment of delegates was based in urban areas on the number of *voters*, in rural areas on the number of *inhabitants*, the ratio of urban voters to rural inhabitants appearing generally as 1 to 5, a ratio which ensured a preponderance of urban representatives in the Congresses of Soviets at all levels.

For example, town soviets were represented in the All-Union Congress of Soviets on the basis of one deputy per 25,000 voters; rural areas, on the other hand, were represented by one deputy for each 125,000 inhabitants, elected by the *Guberniya* Congress of Soviets. In urban areas voting took place by production units, *i.e.* at election meetings in factories, shops, mines, etc., and in rural areas by villages, *i.e.* on a territorial basis. Although the Constitution did not define the method of voting, there was, in practice, no secret ballot, voting being usually by show of hands. Though this has been explained in Soviet sources[1] by the widespread illiteracy of the time, the real motive behind the practice of open voting was clearly less innocuous; and the opportunities it offered for abuse have been officially admitted.[2]

Certain categories of citizens, automatically regarded as class enemies of the régime, were denied electoral rights under the 1918 and 1924 Constitutions. These were: individuals who had had recourse to hired labour for the purpose of profit; private traders and middlemen living on unearned incomes; monks and ministers of religion; employees and agents of the former police, gendarmerie and political police, and members of the Russian royal house.[3] At the same time aliens resident in the Soviet Union enjoyed the franchise on equal terms with Soviet citizens; and discrimination on the basis of race, religion or sex was forbidden by law.

Much of this was changed by the Constitution of 1936, which for the first time introduced universal adult suffrage. The vote was given to 'all citizens of the USSR who have reached the age of 18, irrespective of race or nationality, sex, religion, education, domicile, social origin, property status or past activities.' The only exceptions now are 'persons legally recognised to be insane'.[4] Resident aliens were thus no longer given the vote; while disenfranchised categories of Soviet citizens ceased to exist. The age of eligibility for election to the federal Supreme Soviet was also given as 18, but by an edict of the Presidium of the Supreme Soviet of October 10, 1945, this was raised to 23[5]; by a similar edict exactly a year later the age of eligibility for election to the Supreme Soviets of the Union and autonomous republics was raised to 21.[6] It is interesting to note that until saner judgment prevailed, Soviet jurists used to boast of the absence of any distinction in the Soviet Union between the right to elect and the right to be elected.[7] Experience apparently suggested the desirability of having maturer deputies in the Supreme Soviets. Eighteen remains the age of eligibility for election to local soviets.

The 1936 Constitution proclaims that the soviets at all levels 'are chosen by the electors on the basis of universal, equal and direct suffrage by secret ballot' (Article 134). To test the truth of this statement, it is necessary to examine, in particular, the system of conducting elections, the method of nominating candidates for election and the actual voting procedure.

Responsibility for drawing up the electoral register rests with the Executive Committee (*Ispolkom*) of the village, settlement or town Soviet, or, in the case of towns with a *raion* division, of the appropriate *raion* Soviets. The registers must be displayed for public inspection thirty days before the elections, in order that any necessary changes may be reported and recorded. Appeals against non-inclusion or other faults in the electoral register are addressed to the *Ispolkom*, which must examine the complaint within three days. If the complainant is dissatisfied with the subsequent decision of the *Ispolkom* he may appeal to the People's Court, the lowest unit of the Soviet judicial system, whose decision, which again must be given within three days, is final.[8] A citizen changing his residence permanently or temporarily during this period may obtain a 'Certificate of Right to Vote' enabling him, on presentation of the certificate and proof of identity, to vote wherever he happens to be on the day of the elections.

From 1945 until the 1966 elections the armed forces stationed abroad were represented in both chambers of the USSR Supreme Soviet by deputies elected from special military constituencies in accordance with an edict of October 14, 1945. The special military constituencies were abolished by an edict of March 19, 1966, which established that the armed forces' vote be included in the ordinary constituencies.

Elections take place in single-member constituencies or electoral districts (*okruga*), which for purposes of convenience may be divided into smaller units or wards (*uchastki*). The number of constituencies for elections to local soviets and to the Supreme Soviets of Union and Autonomous Republics is determined by the norms of representation provided in the Constitutions of the Republics. In the case of the bicameral Federal Supreme Soviet the constituencies are drawn up by its Presidium on the basis of Articles 34 and 35 of the USSR Constitution. These state that elections to the Council of the Union shall be conducted on the basis of one deputy for every 300,000 of the population, and elections to the Council of Nationalities on the basis of 32 deputies for each Union Republic, 11 deputies for each Autonomous Republic, 5 deputies for each autonomous *oblast* and one deputy for each national *okrug*.

This means that in elections to the Supreme Soviet of the

[37]

USSR each voter casts his vote in two constituencies of different sizes, or, if he lives in an autonomous area (Autonomous Republic, autonomous *oblast* or national *okrug*), in three. Thus a voter in an Autonomous Republic would cast votes, at the same polling station and at the same time, for deputies to represent him (1) in the Council of the Union; (2) in the Council of Nationalities as an inhabitant of a Union Republic, and (3) in the Council of Nationalities as an inhabitant of an Autonomous Republic. The various votes are distinguished by ballot forms of different colours. In local elections an even greater plurality of votes may occur. Thus, since all local elections take place at the same time, voters living in the town of Karachaevsk, in the Karachaevo-Cherkess Autonomous *Oblast* of the Stavropol *Krai*, would receive four ballot forms to elect deputies to (*a*) the town soviet; (*b*) the soviet of the *raion* to which the town is subordinate; (*c*) the soviet of the autonomous *oblast*, and (*d*) the *krai* soviet.

ELECTORAL COMMISSIONS

The conduct of elections is entrusted to Electoral Commissions, recruited by taking representatives from a list almost identical with that of organisations which are given the right to nominate election candidates, namely professional organisations of workers and employees; co-operative organisations; Communist Party organisations; youth organisations; cultural technical and scientific societies, and other public organisations and societies of the working people, and also meetings of workers and employees by enterprises, of Servicemen by units, meetings of peasants by collective farms and villages and of State farm workers and employees by State farms.[9] At the meetings held to appoint members of the electoral commissions the Communist activists can be expected to ensure the unimpeachable political reliability of those chosen.

For elections to the Supreme Soviet of the USSR the following Electoral Commissions are formed. First, there is a Central Electoral Commission, with supervisory powers to ensure observance of the electoral Statute throughout the USSR, which examines and gives final decisions on complaints about irregularities in the activity of lower electoral commissions, decides on the ballot boxes and ballot forms to be used, registers elected deputies, and finally hands over all relevant

[38]

documentation to the Mandate Commissions of the two Chambers of the Supreme Soviet. In addition, Electoral Commissions with supervisory powers within their own area are set up: (1) in each Union and Autonomous Republic, autonomous *oblast* and national *okrug* for elections to the Council of Nationalities; (2) in the separate electoral districts or constituencies for elections to the two Chambers, and (3) in each election ward (*uchastok*), which is common for elections to both Chambers. The ward electoral commission's main duties are to ensure that all eligible to vote are included in the register and informed of the time and place of voting, to count the votes cast and to present the documentation on the results to the respective constituency Electoral Commission. The constituency Electoral Commission establishes the election result for the constituency, issues certificates of election to the successful candidates and then hands over the relevant documentation to the Central Electoral Commission.[10]

NOMINATION OF CANDIDATES

Article 141 of the USSR Constitution states that the 'right to nominate candidates is secured to public organisations and societies of the working people: Communist Party organisations, trade unions, co-operatives, youth organisations and cultural societies.' The electoral regulations extend this list to include assemblies of workers and other employees at their place of work, collective farmers and State farm workers on their farms, and Servicemen in their units. It is noteworthy that the right to nominate candidates is specifically confined to such groups and organisations, in which, by virtue of the provisions of Article 126 of the Constitution, the Communist Party can exercise a controlling influence. Conversely, a Soviet university textbook[11] has explained that

'in the USSR it would be inexpedient for individuals to have the right of directly nominating candidates: firstly, citizens of the USSR have every opportunity of proposing this or that candidate at general meetings of collectives of working people or through the organs of public organisations; secondly, the proposing of candidates by collectives testifies to the high level of development of organised public opinion in the Soviet State.'

The nominations are sifted at 'pre-election constituency conferences' of representatives of the various collectives which

[39]

have nominated candidates and which, it is agreed, always produce one satisfactory candidate.[12] The registration of only one candidate per constituency is claimed to reflect the 'moral-political unity of Soviet society'.[13]

This aspect of their elections even Soviet citizens must find difficult to describe as democratic. The frequency of the official apologia of the single-candidate system suggests a need to counter popular doubts on the subject: at the very least, it indicates that the logic of the official argument does not suggest itself immediately to the citizen. A booklet, issued in connexion with the 1958 elections to the USSR Supreme Soviet, contains the stock defence of the single-candidate system, which, at the same time, reveals official Soviet sensitivity to foreign criticism:

'In their anti-Soviet propaganda bourgeois ideologists, politicians and propagandists point out, as most important evidence of the anti-democratic nature of the Soviet system, the fact that in the USSR there exists only one party and at the elections to the Soviets only one candidature is put on the voting list in each electoral constituency . . .

'The operative Statutes on Elections in our country do not preclude the right and possibility of nominating and registering several candidates in a constituency. But, in accordance with the practice which has developed, Party and other public organisations and societies of working people, after putting forward candidatures and discussing them thoroughly at meetings, subsequently reach agreement on nominating a single common candidate for a given constituency. He alone is registered in the constituency . . .'[14]

The operative words are 'in accordance with the practice which has developed'—a vague expression that betrays the absence of any cogent justification and, moreover, in view of the official pressures inseparably associated with a totalitarian régime, cannot fail to suggest to the outside observer that such a practice, far from reflecting popular consent, is imposed by official design.

Since Khrushchev's departure, the possibility of allowing more than one candidate in elections has very tentatively been raised on a few isolated occasions, most notably by Arutyunyan, Chairman of the Presidium of the Armenian Supreme Soviet, who argued that:

'putting up more than one candidate in an electoral district, while in no way violating the unity of the electors, would raise their

[40]

political activeness and arouse in the candidate, and then in the deputy, a feeling of responsibility towards the electors.'[15]

So far there have been no reactions to this proposal, and no sign of any attempt to implement it. The obvious difficulty is that it would upset the existing procedure for voting (*see below*, p. 43).

A selected candidate must be formally registered at a session of the Constituency Electoral Commission, and the procedure represents a further step in the process of ensuring his reliability. The members of the commission, as has been already indicated, are themselves chosen in a way that guarantees as far as possible their political loyalty, whether they are Communists or not. The all-important secretary of the commission is almost invariably a Party member. During the 1966 elections to the USSR Supreme Soviet the Secretary of the Central Electoral Commission was I. V. Kapitonov, *cadres* chief of the Party Central Committee. The Secretary of the RSFSR Electoral Commission was Kapitonov's deputy, N. A. Voronovsky. Articles 66 and 67 of the Statute on Elections to the USSR Supreme Soviet stipulate that if the Constituency Electoral Commission refuses to register a candidate, an appeal may be lodged within two days: in the case of elections to the Council of Unions—to the Central Electoral Commission; in the case of elections to the Council of Nationalities—to the Electoral Commission of the appropriate national territory and then, if necessary, to the Central Electoral Commission. The decision of the last-named is final; so that any appeal against irregularities in the registering of candidates cannot proceed beyond the Party-dominated electoral administration.

There can be no recourse to court action by the plaintiff. In these circumstances the chances are remote that any person will be finally accepted as a candidate for election unless his political reliability is assured beyond doubt.

Indeed, election to the soviets is traditionally represented as an honour bestowed in recognition of loyalty to the régime. As a result, candidates elected to the USSR Supreme Soviet, for example, are usually people who have distinguished themselves in various fields, from milkmaids and coal miners to scientists, Marshals of the Soviet Union and industrial managers. In the words of a Soviet pamphlet:

'Soviet people elect to the soviets the finest sons and daughters of the Socialist Motherland, who have merited this honour by their social and labour activity, by their active participation in economic and cultural construction, in the struggle for the victory of Communism.'[16]

All candidates for election in the USSR are presented as members of the 'electoral bloc of Communists and non-Party people'; and in the lists of candidates published in the Press before the elections, membership or otherwise of the Communist Party is not indicated. The idea of this bloc was devised as part of the Communist Party's electoral policy for the first elections to the Supreme Soviet under the new Constitution, in 1937. This further device to eliminate the possibility of effective opposition to the Communist Party's political hegemony was justified by the 'moral-political unity of the Soviet people', following the elimination of antagonistic classes and the victory of Socialism. This line of reasoning was an extension of Stalin's casuistic argument that different political parties necessarily represent different conflicting class interests.

As it is, the existence of the 'bloc of Communists and non-Party people' is presented in official propaganda as proof of popular support:

'The unity of the Party and the people is manifested especially clearly during the time of elections to organs of State power, when the ruling party comes forward in a bloc, in an electoral alliance with all non-Party people.'[17]

The practical value of the arrangement lies in the fact that all candidates must have Party support before they can be registered. By virtue of the Party's directing rôle, the soviets are composed entirely of Party-sponsored or Party-approved deputies. The effectiveness of Party control was demonstrated by the results of the first elections to the USSR Supreme Soviet held in December, 1937. No fewer than 81 per cent of the deputies elected to the Council of the Union and 71 per cent of those elected to the Council of Nationalities were Party members.

As one Soviet book puts it:

'This was the first test of the idea of an electoral bloc of Communists and non-Party people.
'It was a genuine triumph for the Communist Party, a genuine expression of the will of the whole Soviet people ...'[18]

The order of priorities is clear.

It is a peculiarity of Soviet elections that, in addition to the real candidates nominated on the basis of one per constituency, there are often other nominees, prominent Party or Government figures, whose names are put forward for purely honorary reasons in many constituencies. Their names are ultimately withdrawn from all but their customary constituency, leaving only one official candidate in each. That such a neat result is obtained shows clearly that the nominating bodies are instructed in advance who is to be the real candidate.

Further evidence that nominations are prearranged is shown by the fact that the increase or decrease in the number of constituencies for which a national figure is nominated can invariably be taken as an indication of the degree of official favour he currently enjoys. Bulganin, out of favour with his more powerful colleagues, was nominated by only ten constituencies before the 1958 Supreme Soviet elections; Khrushchev was nominated by 136.

Similarly, the number of nominations senior Politburo members received in the 1966 elections, as reported by *Pravda* and *Izvestiya*, was a useful indication of their relative standing: Brezhnev 46; Kosygin 26; Podgorny 17.

VOTING PROCEDURE

On paper, the formal provisions to ensure secrecy of the ballot are irreproachable. Voting takes place on a Sunday, from 6 a.m. to 10 p.m. When the voter enters the polling station he presents to the secretary or an authorised member of the Ward Electoral Commission his passport, collective-farmer's book, trade union card or some other form of identification. After his name has been ticked on the electoral register he receives, in elections to the USSR Supreme Soviet, two ballot papers, for elections to the two chambers of the Supreme Soviet, or, if he lives in an Autonomous republic, autonomous *oblast* or national *okrug*, three ballot papers. Each ballot paper contains the candidate's name, the name of the organisation that nominated him and the fact that he is a member of the Party, if such is the case. Provision is made on the ballot paper for a choice of candidates, for each paper also bears instructions to the voter to leave the name of the candidate for whom he is voting and to 'cross out the rest'. The polling station must be provided with special rooms or booths where the voter may retire alone to complete his ballot papers. He then folds the papers and drops them into sealed boxes.

If it were obligatory for a voter to follow out this procedure, there could be little criticism of the system, at any rate on the score of secrecy. Unfortunately, theory and practice once more part company. As has been stated, Soviet practice is not to provide a choice of candidates on the ballot paper, but to enter the name of only one candidate, whom the voter may either accept or reject. The crucial point is that the ballot paper is valid without marking, since it bears only one name. If there were two candidates it would be necessary to use the booths provided to cross out the name of one of them. As it is, the voters' only reason for using the booth would be to cross out the name of the officially-sponsored candidate.

The practice of all but the more reckless citizens is thus to fold the ballot paper and drop it into the box without entering the screened voting booth. In view of the scrupulous, and even pedantic, enforcement of all the other requirements of electoral procedure, it is, to say the least, odd that there should be no insistence on the voter going through the forms of secret election. This form of open voting, which is, strictly speaking, a violation of the regulations, is not only not officially discouraged but is rather viewed as an act of civic loyalty. Thus the Soviet voter is subjected to moral pressure, which is intensified by the fact that all the media of communication and propaganda are employed to press the elector into casting his vote in approved Party fashion. It requires more courage than the average Soviet voter is prepared to display to reveal public opposition. In practice, therefore, there is no secret ballot in the sense in which that term is understood in the free world.

Nevertheless, the absence of alternative candidates does not mean that the official candidate is automatically elected. Soviet propaganda makes much of the regulation that, to be elected, a candidate must obtain an absolute majority of the votes cast; the election is only valid if more than half the electorate cast their votes.

But such circumstances occur very infrequently. In the March, 1965, elections to local soviets of the RSFSR, for example, at which 1,059,255 deputies were elected only 170 candidates failed to obtain[19] the necessary absolute majority of votes, and only 1,873 ballot papers were declared invalid.

[44]

When a candidate fails to be elected a new ballot must be held within two weeks, according to the Statutes on Elections. Unfortunately, the electoral regulations are based on the assumption of a choice of candidates in the same constituency. Thus, Article 125 of the Statute on Elections to local soviets of the RSFSR states that if no one candidate obtains an absolute majority of the votes cast, a re-ballot shall be taken within two weeks on the 'two candidates who obtained the highest number of votes'. Since, in practice, there is never more than one candidate per constituency one can only conjecture how the re-ballot is taken if the candidate fails to obtain an absolute majority by virtue of having too many votes cast against him (as distinct from a less than 50 per cent poll, which would automatically result in demands for a fresh election). Presumably he is replaced by another candidate; but this contingency is not covered by the regulations.

Perhaps the most impressive aspect of Soviet elections is the almost incredibly high poll invariably recorded. Provision is made for a voter to cast his ballot wherever he may be, on a transcontinental train, aboard a ship at sea or in a hospital bed. There are hardly any physical obstacles to prevent a 100 per cent vote in most areas of the Soviet Union. The following figures show the percentages voting in elections to the USSR Supreme Soviet under the new Constitution: 1937—96·8; 1946—99·7; 1950—99·98; 1954—99·98; 1958—99·97; 1962—99·95; 1966—99·94.

As the only candidates permitted to stand, the 'bloc of Communists and non-Party people' must obtain a high proportion of the votes. As one Soviet journal put it, with unconscious irony, 'no bourgeois party has, or can have, such success in the elections'.[20] But the absurdity of Soviet election claims can be seen clearly from the fact that the various nationalities which were deported en bloc from their own areas during and shortly after the war were stated at the previous elections to have voted almost unanimously for the Soviet régime. The Volga Germans are an example. Ninety-nine point eight per cent of them had voted in the 1938 elections to the Republican Supreme Soviets, 99·7 for the official candidates. They were accused three years later of harbouring 'tens of thousands of diversionists and spies'[21] and deported to other areas of the Soviet Union.

If, as has been suggested, the results of Soviet elections are largely a foregone conclusion, it is legitimate to ask why the authorities should consider it worthwhile to incur such tremendous expense, in money and man-power, to achieve it. The truth is that the choice of deputies for the representative bodies is virtually a secondary feature. The main purpose is to provide the setting for a contrived demonstration of popular support for the régime. Elections are conducted in a festive atmosphere reminiscent of the May Day and Revolution anniversary holidays, with flags, banners, music and portraits of the leaders. Like May Day and the Revolution anniversary, too, they are made the pretext for production drives during which workers pledge themselves 'in honour of the elections' to overfulfil their output norms. All the media of communication and information are exploited to enumerate the achievements of the régime in domestic and foreign affairs, which are presented as the 'fruits of the wise Leninist policy of the Communist Party'.[22] The electorate are repeatedly reminded that

'by voting for the candidates of the bloc of Communists and non-Party people, our people—the all-powerful masters of the country—will be voting for the Leninist policy of the Communist Party—the policy of the victorious construction of a Communist society in our land.'[23]

The aim of this high-powered propaganda is to get as many people as possible not only to participate in elections but to do so as a conscious public affirmation of support for the régime. This is psychologically important; it preserves the fiction of democracy while identifying the people with the Party and, by implication, committing them to its policies.

After the elections, the propaganda campaign continues, as it were, to drive home the lesson. The inevitable results are now presented as fresh proof of the

'triumph of Soviet Socialist democracy, the unity and cohesion of the peoples of the USSR around the Communist Party and its Leninist Central Committee, the complete and undivided victory of the people's bloc of Communists and non-Party people.'[24]

An election provides a dramatic occasion for creating an illusion of mass participation in State affairs, even though those taking part can have little influence on the final outcome. The machinery for nominating, registering and polling entails the enlistment throughout the country of millions of people. Eight and three-quarter million were employed in Electoral Commissions alone during the 1965 elections to the local Soviets.[25]

An election also provides a valuable opportunity for Party workers and helpers to practise their skill as agitators in 'selling' the régime to the electorate. It was claimed, for example, that during the 1955 local elections 14 to 15 million people were employed in this capacity.[26] This exploitation of elections illustrates the considerable skill shown by the ruling *élite* in using the trappings of mass democracy to mask the dictatorial nature of the régime.

THE ELECTED CANDIDATES

The official indication of the nature of the end product of the elaborate electoral campaign appears in the reports of the Mandate Commissions to the soviets at their opening sessions. In the USSR Supreme Soviet the Mandate Commissions of the Council of the Union and the Council of Nationalities present their analyses of the new membership separately to the respective chambers. The information given in them includes: membership of one or other of the recognised social classes, possession of honours or decorations, Party membership or candidate status, sex, age and education, and also a breakdown of the membership according to nationality—an analysis designed to demonstrate the 'genuinely popular character of the Soviet Parliament'.[27]

In the USSR Supreme Soviet elected in June, 1966, 46 per cent of the deputies of the Supreme Soviet were shown as being workers and peasants by employment. The rest were members of the intelligentsia.

Since the duties of the USSR Supreme Soviet are, in practice, narrowly formal, and membership is regarded largely as a reward for services to the régime, it is not surprising that a high proportion of its members are holders of decorations and honours (77 per cent in the Supreme Soviet elected in 1966). By the same token, one finds a high proportion of members or candidate-members of the Communist Party (75 per cent). In the local soviets as a whole the proportion of Party members is 45·2 per cent.[28] It declines markedly the lower down the scale of Soviets one goes. In the Supreme Soviets of the Republics

[47]

it is 68 per cent.[29] It also varies considerably from Republic to Republic. But even at the lower levels, i.e., below that of *oblast* and *krai*, a high proportion of Deputies are Party members— in 1966, in the Minsk *oblast* of Byelorussia, for instance, over 40 per cent.[30]

It has been noted that in both central and local soviets there is a fairly rapid turnover of members. For example, of the deputies elected to the USSR Supreme Soviet in 1966 about 67 per cent were new; among the 1,059,255 deputies elected to local soviets in the RSFSR in 1965, 58·8 per cent were new.

The soviets are traditionally regarded as schools of administration, and this has been offered as an explanation of such a rapid turnover. This may hold good for the local soviets, service in which probably does provide a training in low-level leadership, possibly eventually resulting in promotion. On the other hand, most members of the Supreme Soviet are already highly placed in the Government, Party or managerial hierarchies and are not likely to gain further experience from the extremely limited glimpse of Government work provided by that body. A more probable explanation is the desire of the régime to give the widest possible number of people a sense of having participated in the running of the country's administration and thus to create an impression of mass representation and control in public affairs.

SOURCES

1. Askerov *et al.*, p. 316.
2. Vyshinsky, p. 693.
3. Askerov *et al.*, p. 316.
4. Article 135 of the USSR Constitution: *Sotsialisticheskaya Zakonnost*, No. 1, 1959.
5. *Sbornik Zakonov SSSR i Ukazov Prezidiuma Verkhovnogo Soveta SSSR,* 1945–6, p. 38.
6. *Ibid.*, p. 57.
7. Vyshinsky, p. 678.
8. *Polozheniye o Vyborakh v Verkhovny Sovet SSSR,* 1966, arts. 21–23.
9. *Ibid.*, art. 36.
10. *Ibid*, chapter 5.
11. Askerov *et al.*, p. 324.
12. *Ibid.*, p. 325.
13. Starovoitov, p. 19.
14. Filonovich, pp. 27–8.
15. *Kommunist* (of Armenia), March 5, 1966.
16. Filonovich, p. 3.
17. Mamontov, p. 26.
18. *Ibid.*, p. 31.
19. *Sovetskaya Rossiya*, March 19, 1965.
20. *Sovety Deputatov Trudyashchikhsya, No.* 1, 1958, *p.* 12.
21. *Vedomosti Verkhovnogo Soveta SSSR, No.* 38, 1941.
22. *Pravda*, March 17, 1958.
23. *Pravda*, March 15, 1958.
24. *Pravda*, March 19, 1958.

25. *Pravda*, March 28, 1965.
26. Scott, p. 97.
27. *Zasedaniya Verkhovnogo Soveta SSSR Pyatogo Sozyva (Pervaya Sessiya) Stenograficheski Otchet*, p. 162.

28. *Kommunist*, No. 8, 1966, p. 81.
29. *Osnovy Sovetskogo Gosudarstvennogo Stroitelstva i Prava*, p. 234.
30. *Partiinaya Zhizn*, No. 5, 1966, p. 33.

IV

The Supreme Soviets

Under the 1936 Constitution (Article 30) the USSR Supreme Soviet is declared to be the 'highest organ of State power in the USSR'. It has the exclusive right to legislate for the USSR (Article 32), and exercises all the federal powers either alone or through the federal organs accountable to it, *i.e.* the Presidium of the USSR Supreme Soviet, the USSR Council of Ministers and the Ministries of the USSR (Article 31). Thus, constitutionally, the Supreme Soviet is invested with the powers of a democratic parliament.

ELECTION AND DISSOLUTION

The Supreme Soviet is elected by universal suffrage for a term of four years (the norms of representation for the two chambers are given in the chapter on the Electoral System). Theoretically, numerical equality between the two Chambers is regarded as desirable. In his report on the draft Constitution of 1936 to the Extraordinary Eighth Congress of Soviets, Stalin referred with approval to a proposed addendum to the draft Constitution calling for an equal number of members in both Chambers. This, he said, had 'obvious political advantage, for it emphasises the equality of the Chambers'.[1] But the Constitution as it stands does not specifically provide for such numerical equality; nor could it do, because whereas representation in the Council of Nationalities is more or less constant, except for infrequent minor changes caused by adjustments in the status of national territories; representation in the Council of the Union will continue to change with the rise in population. The two Chambers in the Supreme Soviet of 1937, the first to be elected under the new Constitution, were almost equal in numbers, with 569 deputies in the Council of the Union and 574 in the Council of Nationalities.

Since then the Council of the Union has significantly outnumbered the Council of Nationalities, and the increase in the number of its deputies has even outstripped that which would be warranted by the population increase. In the Supreme Soviet elected in 1962, membership of the Chambers was, respectively, 791 and 652. In the 1966 elections, however, the Council of the Union was reduced to 767 deputies (its proper size, according to the constitutional requirement of one deputy per 300,000 of the population), and the Council of Nationalities was increased to 750 deputies by raising the representation of the Union Republics from 25 to 32 per Republic.

On the expiry of the four-year term of office of the Supreme Soviet, or in the event of its being dissolved by its Presidium in accordance with the Constitutional provision concerning disagreement between the two Chambers (a contingency which has never arisen), the Presidium is required to fix the election of a new Supreme Soviet within two months from the date of expiry of office or the dissolution of the previous Supreme Soviet. This provision has not in practice been strictly observed. For instance the 1966 elections were well over three weeks later than required under the Constitution. The newly-elected Supreme Soviet must be convened by the outgoing Presidium, not later than three months after the elections. (Articles 54 and 55 of the Constitution.)

ORGANISATION AND PROCEDURE

Regular sessions of the Supreme Soviet are, according to the Constitution, convened twice a year, and extraordinary sessions may be convened by the Presidium at its own discretion or at the request of one of the Union Republics (Article 46). Since Stalin's death there has been a sustained campaign to invest the Supreme Soviet with an appearance of authority and respectability, and regular sessions have been held, on an average twice a year, although not literally within the prescribed limits. The second session of the Supreme Soviet of the fourth convocation, scheduled for the second half of 1954, did not take place until February of the following year. The sixth session, scheduled for the second half of 1956, was similarly delayed. In both cases events showed that the main business of the sessions had been the subject of dispute within the Party Presidium and Central Committee, and the convening of what is theoretically the supreme organ of power in the USSR was delayed until these Party disputes were resolved. Nevertheless, matters have improved since Stalin's day: from 1947 until his death the Supreme Soviet was never convened more than once a year.

Sessions of the Supreme Soviet are brief, lasting usually three or four days and hardly ever more than a week. The seventh and ninth sessions, *i.e.*, the two final regular sessions of the fourth convocation (held in May and December, 1957, respectively) for example, took up only seven days between them. The first session of the fifth convocation, in March, 1958, worked for only 3½ days. The brevity of sessions is regarded as evidence of the superiority of the Soviet system over that of bourgeois countries, where 'sessions last for several months at a time' because the bourgeoisie is interested in 'turning parliament into a talking-shop for the purpose of deceiving the people'.[2]

The real reason that sessions of the Supreme Soviet are so brief is because of the extremely limited range of State business deputies are permitted to participate in, and also because of the rail-roading of measures which in a truly democratic parliament would meet with resistance. For instance, the edicts of the Presidium passed between sessions are not debated or discussed in the Supreme Soviet but are voted for approval as soon as they have been presented by the Secretary of the Presidium. In this way, what is potentially the Supreme Soviet's most powerful function is reduced to a formality.

Since the two Chambers have equal rights and powers to initiate legislation, and a law can become valid only if passed by a simple majority in each Chamber (Articles 37–39), separate votes of the Chambers are taken on all normative laws (*zakon*). But this does not necessarily involve separate sittings; the deputies of the two Chambers merely vote in turn. In March, 1958, for example, the draft 'Law on the Further Development of the Collective Farm System and the Reorganisation of the MTS', was voted on separately by the two Chambers at a joint sitting.

As a corollary to the equality of the Chambers, the Constitution also provides for the dissolution of the Supreme Soviet and the election of a new one when disagreement between the two Chambers over a matter under consideration is not settled to the satisfaction of both Chambers by a 'Joint Conciliation Commission' (Article 47). No occasion has ever arisen for recourse to this provision. Indeed, as one Soviet author pointed out, with misplaced pride.

'As experience shows, voting is exceptionally unanimous. In the practical work of the USSR Supreme Soviet there has never yet been a single case of any question placed on the agenda of a session being unresolved, as is often the case in the practice of bourgeois parliaments, in particular the British Parliament and the American Congress.'[3]

A notable example of such 'unanimity' occurred on the dramatic occasion in February, 1955, when Malenkov was replaced as Chairman of the Council of Ministers of the USSR by Bulganin. Although the move to replace Malenkov came as a surprise to many of the deputies, not only was there not a single dissenting vote but no one even questioned it.

Similarly, at the December, 1964, session not a single voice was heard questioning the official explanations (old age and ill-health) for the replacement of Khrushchev as Chairman of the Council of Ministers by Kosygin.

Before a session of the Supreme Soviet opens, preliminary planning is carried out by the 'Councils of Elders' of the two Chambers, which consist of senior deputies delegated by the deputy groups from the various Republics and regions. The Councils of Elders are in fact thinly disguised agencies for ensuring Party control of Supreme Soviet proceedings. As a legal textbook puts it:

'In accordance with the constitutional practice which has grown up they [the Councils] work under the direction of the Party group of the USSR Supreme Soviet which consists of deputies who are Party members.'[4]

The Councils recommend candidates for the offices of Chairman and deputy Chairmen to their respective Chambers, and assist in working out the agenda of the session; while most of the proposals concerning the procedure to be adopted, and in regard to elections to or changes in the Presidium of the Supreme Soviet, the office of the Prosecutor-General and the Council of Ministers are put forward in their name.

At the beginning of the first session of a new Supreme Soviet the Chambers meet separately, and, on the recommendation of the Council of Elders, the senior deputy of each Chamber declares the session open. It is he who conducts the election of Chairman of the Chamber, who in turn conducts the elec-

[53]

tion of his four deputies. Henceforth the function of steering business through the Chamber belongs to the Chairman and his deputies.

Between sessions, the posts of the Chairmen of the Chambers involve them in a number of duties, such as the signing of messages to foreign parliaments and a certain amount of organisational work; but they are not full-time officials.

After the approval of the agenda for the session, each Chamber elects its Mandate Commission, including a Chairman. The two Chambers of the Supreme Soviet, like other soviets, verify the credentials of their own members, and it is they who would hear disputes if there were any. In fact, these do not occur.

After election, the Mandate Commissions report back. In the meantime the Supreme Soviet continues its business. In March, 1958, the Mandate Commissions reported back the following day, but, meanwhile the Supreme Soviet had elected the Presidium, approved the work of the outgoing government and formed a new one, heard the main report from Khrushchev and referred it to the Legislative Proposals Commissions of the two Houses. The Mandate Commissions remain in office throughout the term of the Supreme Soviet and report at the beginning of all subsequent sessions on the credentials of any members elected in by-elections.

The other 'permanent commissions' of each Chamber are also elected at separate sittings.

The election of the Presidium of the Supreme Soviet and the appointment of the Chairman of the Council of Ministers take place at a joint session of the two Chambers. In August, 1966, the chairman of the session read out the conventional application from Kosygin, the outgoing Chairman of the Council of Ministers, laying down its powers on the expiry of office in accordance with Article 70 of the Constitution. Then Brezhnev, on behalf of the CPSU Central Committee, proposed Kosygin's reappointment and that he be entrusted with forming a new Government. A decree embodying this proposal was then immediately unanimously adopted. At a second joint session Brezhnev, again on behalf of the CPSU Central Committee, proposed Podgorny as Chairman of the Presidium of the Supreme Soviet. After this had been unanimously approved, Podgorny, on behalf of the Party group of the Supreme Soviet and the Councils of Elders, proposed the other candidatures for the Presidium. These were voted for *en bloc* and approved unanimously. Kosygin then proposed his new Government (which was identical with the outgoing one), not omitting to point out that it had already been approved by the CPSU Central Committee, and this also was approved unanimously.

Discussions in the Supreme Soviet are of a generally low standard. 'Off-the-cuff' debating is unknown; speeches are prepared in advance and lack spontaneity, and it is exceptional for differences of opinion to be aired.

The only type of criticism that is encouraged within limits is that designed to facilitate the implementation of official policy without questioning the policy itself. Individual Ministers may be rebuked, with official sanction; not, however, on the score of the officially-approved policy they are applying but because they are not applying it with sufficient vigour and competence, or, following a policy change, because convenient scapegoats are required.

Even Soviet sources have confessed that some Supreme Soviet deputies regard its sessions as having only ritualistic, not political, importance. An *Izvestiya* report at the end of 1965 said:

'One met, it is true, silent and passive deputies. In their own locality these were energetic and active people, but here they attended silently and solemnly like honorary representatives of the people; it was as if nothing but a ceremonial of power was being exercised and not seething, live, vital acts.'[5]

The Soviet authorities are plainly sensitive to criticism, especially from abroad, of the undignified and passive rôle of the Supreme Soviet in actual session. For this reason the annual debate on the Budget and annual Plan is stage-managed in such a way as to create the impression, among the unsophisticated at any rate, that the Supreme Soviet is not merely a rubber-stamp body. An elaborate drama is enacted to produce the illusion that the deputies are not mere automata, and that the Supreme Soviet is free and able to exercise the same measure of control over the executive as is a genuine democratic Parliament. Reports on the draft annual Plan and on the draft Budget are presented on behalf of the Council of Ministers at a joint sitting by the responsible Ministers. The two Chambers then hold separate sittings to hear the co-reports of their respective Budget Commissions. The *co-rapporteur* in each case praises the achievements of the past year and approves both the draft annual Plan and the draft Budget in principle. He then announces that the Budget Commission has examined the two reports and proposes certain amendments. The amendments invariably favour increased production in the case of the annual Plan, and increased revenue in the case of the Budget. An exact figure is given for the anticipated increased revenue and details of its proposed expenditure.

In December, 1965, for instance, the Budget Commission of the Council of the Union proposed amendments to the draft Budget providing for an increase in revenue of 120·6 million roubles. The same day the Council of Nationalities met and heard the co-report of its own Budget Commission, whose proposals for increased revenues and for their detailed expenditure were identical with those put forward in the Council of the Union. In these circumstances, apart from the obvious improbability of the Party being taken by surprise, it is hard to avoid the conclusion that the supposed amendments were planned in advance. The Government supposedly studies the proposed amendments; but that this is a mere formality is shown by the fact that at the December, 1957, session a final draft of the Budget, containing the amendments proposed by the Budget Commissions, was presented and adopted in the afternoon of the very day on which the amendments were proposed, ostensibly for the first time.

On certain very important matters the authority of the legislature has appeared to count for little. This applies notably to the Five-Year Plans. The Fourth Five-Year Plan (1946–50) was approved by the Supreme Soviet and embodied in a law.[6] The abandoned Sixth Five-Year Plan was also scheduled, under a resolution of the December, 1956, Central Committee plenum, to be submitted for the approval of the Supreme Soviet.[7] The intervening Fifth Five-Year Plan, however, which ran its full course from 1951 to 1955, was endorsed (two years after commencement) only by the Party Congress, in October, 1952.[8] It was never submitted to the Supreme Soviet, although, of course, the financial provisions were examined annually in the Budget. To be embodied in law a Five-Year Plan must obviously be submitted to the Supreme Soviet; but non-observance of this formality does not appear to have invalidated the Plan in practice.

On occasions a theme which is to provide one of the propaganda keynotes of the session may be introduced, ostensibly as a surprise to the Government, in the form of a question from a group of deputies. Such a question must be answered, under Article 71 of the Constitution, within three days. In February, 1957, an inspired question of this kind enabled Mikhailov, Minister of Culture, to set forth once again, during the foreign policy debate, the Soviet Government's views on cultural contacts, and to suggest that all the difficulties in that sphere derived from the deliberate obstructionism of Western leaders. In December, 1965, three questions on foreign policy provided the Minister, Gromyko, with a pretext for making a long speech attacking the United States' and West German Governments. The speech was then debated and this served as the basis for the adoption of a Decree endorsing the Soviet Government's foreign policy. The questions so far put forward in the Supreme Soviet have been so framed as to provide convenient propaganda pegs for official policy, and, in the circumstances, it would be unwarranted and naïve to suggest that they serve any more useful purpose.

COMMISSIONS OF THE SUPREME SOVIET

Commissions of the Supreme Soviet may be formed on a permanent or on a temporary basis. The Constitution itself empowers the Supreme Soviet to appoint commissions of investigation and inspection whenever it sees fit, and obliges institutions and officials to comply with their demands and provide them with the materials and documents they require (Article 51). These are *ad hoc* commissions set up to inquire into specific matters, and their term of service ends on completion of their immediate task.

More important in the day-to-day business of the Supreme Soviet are the so-called permanent commissions of the two Chambers, which remain in operation throughout the term of office of the Supreme Soviet. At the first session of the seventh convocation, in August, 1966, they were increased from four in the Council of the Union and five in the Council of Nationalities to ten for each Chamber. Each Chamber elected, in addition to its Mandate Commission, Commissions for: foreign affairs; planning and budget; legislative proposals; industry, transport and communications; construction and construction materials; agriculture; health and social welfare; education, science and culture; trade and everyday services. The number of members in each Commission varies from 31 to 51. This adds up to a sizeable figure: 700 out of the total of 1,517 deputies are included in the Commissions. The Commissions are elected from among the deputies of the respective Chambers, and it is the Chambers which determine their size. They are responsible to the Chamber that elected them, and, in between sessions of the Supreme Soviet, are accountable to the Chairman of the Chamber. In practice, however, most of their activity appears to be coordinated by the Presidium of the Supreme Soviet.[9] Plenary meetings are held as required, but not less than once every three months; and members have the right of leave of absence from their ordinary jobs for the period of the meetings.[10]

The organisation and procedure of the Legislative Proposals Commissions are defined in special statutes adopted by the respective Chambers in February, 1947; that of the other permanent Commissions is stated to be analogous.[11] The presence of two-thirds of the membership constitutes a quorum, and decisions are taken by simple majority vote. Members disagreeing with adopted decisions have, in principle, the right to defend their point of view during subsequent discussion in the Chamber. Deputies of either Chamber who are not members of the Commissions may attend meetings and take part in the discussion, but without the right to vote.

The permanent Commissions have as their task the preliminary examination and elaboration of draft legislative proposals which are to be submitted for confirmation by the Supreme Soviet. Draft State economic plans and budgets must be examined by the Commission, but apart from this there are no rules establishing which draft proposals may or may not come before the Commissions. In practice it is the Presidium of the Supreme Soviet which decides what they deal with. Of 241 laws adopted by the 6th convocation of the Supreme Soviet (elected in 1962) before its 7th session, only 53 had come before the Commissions. Only on one occasion has a draft proposal been examined by a Commission upon the request of the Supreme Soviet itself.[12]

The Budget Commissions are primarily concerned with studying the annual Plan and the State Budget and reporting their conclusions and proposed amendments during the debate on the drafts in their respective Chambers (see p. 55). They may also examine and report on other draft laws containing

[58]

financial and budgetary provisions.[13] The Foreign Affairs Commissions submit to their respective Chambers their conclusions on draft laws concerning the foreign policy of the State, and present to the Supreme Soviet or its Presidium their conclusions on matters concerning the ratification, denunciation or annulment of treaties and agreements concluded with foreign States. The Legislative Proposals Commissions concern themselves with draft laws of a general character, those, in fact, which do not come within the more specialised purview of the Budget and Foreign Affairs Commissions. All these three types of permanent Commission also have the right of legislative initiative and may themselves draw up and submit for consideration of the Supreme Soviet draft laws on matters within their competence.[14]

All the permanent commissions are authorised to consult and require information from State and public institutions and from individual experts. They may also set up sub-committees, either to facilitate the detailed and expert examination of draft legislative proposals or, in the case of those Commissions which have the power of legislative initiative, to prepare initial versions of draft laws. These sub-committees, which are usually headed by members of the appropriate permanent Commissions, may include Supreme Soviet deputies (who may or may not be members of the Commissions), representatives of Ministries and departments, or individual scholars versed in the relevant field of study.[15] The aid of the public may also be enlisted by the publication of draft laws for general discussion. An example was the publication in the legal journals, by the Legislative Proposals Commissions of the two Chambers, of drafts of the proposed basic principles of criminal legislation and procedure, on which readers were invited to submit their observations and suggestions to the Commissions.[16]

The procedures of the permanent Commissions and of their *ad hoc* sub-committees do not appear in any official bulletin, so that it is impossible to discover to what extent divergent views are expressed and divisions of opinion recorded. Only the final recommendations of the permanent Commissions are published in the proceedings of the Supreme Soviet. But with their right to initiate legislation and their power to influence the Supreme Soviet in its assessment of proposed legislation, it is not inconceivable that the permanent Commissions could, in theory at least, disrupt Party policy.

[59]

They are insured against this most unlikely contingency, however, by the presence in their midst of a disproportionate number of Party *apparatchiki* and members of the higher Party organs, and by being placed under the Chairmanship of Party functionaries. Thus, in seven of the ten permanent Commissions of the Council of the Union elected in August, 1966, the Chairman is a full member of the CPSU Central Committee; in one a candidate member; in one a member of the Central Committee's Revision Commission; and only one (the health commission) is not presided over by a senior Party functionary. A large proportion of the members of all Commissions are either local *apparatchiki*, usually *oblast* Party Secretaries, or members and candidate-members of the Party Central Committee. The Commissions of the Council of Nationalities are less packed with Party functionaries but six of the ten are presided over by members or candidate-members of the CPSU Central Committee.

Of the remainder of the members of the permanent Commissions of both Chambers who are not either full-time Party officials or members of the higher organs of the Party, the majority are relatively high-powered Government personnel whose standing in Party esteem must be high. The number of workers and peasants in the permanent Commissions of the Supreme Soviet is, on the other hand, extremely small, and in no way commensurate with their representation in the Supreme Soviet itself. Even allowing for the perhaps specialised knowledge and experience needed by members of the permanent Commissions, this is a state of affairs hard to reconcile with the traditional view of the soviets as schools of administration: it suggests, on the contrary, that in those phases of State business in which policy tends to be discussed, as distinct from those in which it is merely applied, the Party takes considerable precautions to ensure that its interests are strongly represented.

DUTIES AND RIGHTS OF DEPUTIES

The Supreme Soviet deputy, it is emphasised in official propaganda, is the 'servant of the people, the representative of the working people in the organs of State power',[17] who is required by law to report regularly to his constituents on his own activity and that of the Soviet (Article 142 of the USSR Constitution). It is officially admitted, however, that 'there are among our deputies some who unpardonably forget their duty and obligations', and who, 'having spoken once at the pre-election meeting, no longer see any need to meet the electors, receive visitors only rarely and grudgingly, answer letters formally, and do nothing to carry out the instructions given them'.[18]

The deputy's main functions between sessions of the soviet appear to be two-fold: (1) to explain and propagandise official policy, and (2) to carry out the instructions (*nakazy*) received from constituents and to redress grievances by interceding with the authorities. Of these, the first is by far the more important and is the main reason for official insistence on a close link between deputy and constituents and why stress is laid on his work in the constituency rather than at the centre. An official journal stated that

'A most important obligation of the deputy is his participation in the work of sessions of the Soviet and its organs, the carrying out of the tasks and missions of the Soviet, of its permanent commissions. But despite all this the deputy must remember that the centre of his daily activity is the constituency. Here he is called on to be an active propagandist and executor of the policy of the Party and Government, to bring the Soviet's decisions to the knowledge of the population and organise their fulfilment, to stand on guard over the rights of citizens and to educate the working people in the spirit of respect for the laws of the Soviet State and the rules of Socialist communal living, in the spirit of patriotic fidelity to the Motherland.'[19]

This definition of the deputy's duties clearly precludes the idea of freedom to oppose official policy: his function is confined to ensuring that it is *carried out*.

Since he has the right of access to Ministries and enterprises and can demand information in writing from Ministers, the deputy is in a position to get things done which constituents themselves are hampered from achieving by bureaucracy and lack of information. It is pointed out that the deputy's primary function is that of an organiser; the good deputy organises activists among the population and delegates work to them.[20] For this reason he maintains close contact with assistance committees attached to house administrations, street committees, parents' committees in schools, etc., and arranges as far as possible for tasks to be performed by voluntary public labour.

[61]

In addition, the deputy may be asked by constituents to use his influence with the local authorities to register complaints or grievances of one kind or another. He may be asked to check on whether a retired person's pension has been correctly calculated, to find work for school-leavers in local plants, or to help a man with a large family to find accommodation. Since, moreover, the nature of the problems on which a constituent may consult his deputy has never been clearly defined, there have been frequent complaints from USSR Supreme Soviet deputies that they are repeatedly asked to intercede in matters which should more properly be dealt with at a lower level, *i.e.,* referred to the constituents' deputies in local soviets.

Clearly, the deputy's task is complicated by the fact that he is not a permanent official in the sense of devoting his whole time to parliamentary duties. After election he remains at his ordinary job, which he leaves only to attend the periodic sessions of the soviet. The rest of his duties as a deputy he has to perform in his spare time, in accordance with the Leninist precept that deputies 'must work themselves, execute their own laws, must themselves test their results in real life and be directly responsible to their constituents'.[21] The most likely cause, therefore, of the alleged neglect of their duties by certain deputies is precisely the difficulty of finding time to receive callers, answer correspondence, etc., in a constituency (in the case of deputies in the Council of the Union) of 300,000 people, while holding down a regular job in industry or agriculture. Nevertheless, the system of part-time deputies is claimed by Soviet propagandists to be superior to the 'bourgeois' system of full-time paid Members of Parliament, which, allegedly, leads to corruption and abuse.[22] The natural objection to this line of reasoning is that, since sessions of the USSR Supreme Soviet occur only twice a year and last only a few days, the Soviet deputy does not have the same opportunity as, say, a British MP, of keeping Ministers up to the mark by asking questions week after week and eliciting replies for the public record.

There is one feature of the Soviet parliamentary system which is invariably produced like a trump card by those seeking to prove its superiority over 'bourgeois' systems. This is the constitutionally proclaimed right of constituents to recall a deputy who fails to carry out his duties to their satisfaction. Article 142 of the USSR Constitution states that a deputy 'may be recalled at any time upon the decision of a majority of the electors in the manner established by law'. This again is based on a Leninist precept that

'Any elective institution or assembly of representatives whatsoever can be considered truly democratic and really representative of the popular will only on condition of recognition and use of the right of recall by the electors of their chosen representatives.'[23]

In practice, very little use has been made of the right of recall; and, in view of its prominence in the Soviet propaganda armoury, it is rather odd to note in a Soviet pamphlet[24] that the main reason for this was the absence of any established recall procedure. Only at the end of 1959 did the USSR Supreme Soviet pass a law to remedy the omission.

The USSR Supreme Soviet deputy also enjoys certain privileges. The Constitution guarantees him against prosecution or arrest without the consent of the Supreme Soviet of the USSR or, between sessions, of its Presidium (Article 52). He has the privilege of free transport over the whole public transport system of the USSR, and a monthly salary of 100 roubles 'to meet out-of-pocket expenses'.[25] While on parliamentary duties, he receives his normal average earnings from his place of work, and during sessions of the Supreme Soviet a daily expense allowance.

THE PRESIDIUM OF THE USSR SUPREME SOVIET

The Presidium of the Supreme Soviet came into being on January 17, 1938, at the first session of the Supreme Soviet convened under the 1936 Constitution, in which it is included with the Supreme Soviet as one of the 'higher organs of State power' of the USSR. It consisted of a Chairman, a number of deputy Chairmen, a Secretary, and a number of members. In his report on the new Constitution to the Extraordinary Eighth All-Union Congress of Soviets, Stalin accepted, as enhancing the prestige of the Presidium, a proposed amendment that the number of deputy Chairmen should correspond to the number of Union Republics, at that time eleven. He rejected a proposed addendum to Article 48 of the Constitution that the Chairman of the Presidium should be elected not by the Supreme Soviet but by the people:

'I think this addendum is wrong, because it runs counter to the spirit of our Constitution. According to the system of our Constitu-

[63]

tion, there must not be an individual President in the USSR, elected by the whole population on a par with the Supreme Soviet, and able to put himself in opposition to the Supreme Soviet. The President in the USSR is a collegium, it is the Presidium of the Supreme Soviet, including the Chairman of the Presidium of the Supreme Soviet, elected, not by the whole population but by the Supreme Soviet, and accountable to the Supreme Soviet. Historical experiences shows that such a structure of the supreme bodies is the most democratic, and safeguards the country against undesirable contingencies.'[26]

The Presidium is thus officially conceived as a 'collective President', and its Chairman is deemed to have no distinct powers of his own. Although the laws of the Supreme Soviet and the Edicts of the Presidium are promulgated over his signature, and it is he who accepts the letters of credence of foreign Ambassadors, awards decorations, etc., he acts, it is stated, in the name, and by the collective decision of the whole Presidium.[27] Nevertheless, in practice, it is the Chairman of the Presidium who fulfils all the functions traditionally associated with the titular head of State of a country in its relations with other States. For this reason he is frequently referred to outside the USSR as the Soviet President.

The deputy Chairmen of the Presidium are traditionally the Chairmen of the Presidia of the Supreme Soviets of the Union Republics. It is, however, nowhere suggested in Soviet sources that one position is held *ex officio* by virtue of the other. Since, in any case, election to the two offices rests with two different bodies, it would be difficult, in theory, to ensure that the same man occupied both. Under the Soviet political system, however, the task of engineering this neat pattern appears to offer little difficulty in practice.

The Presidium now consists of the Chairman, 15 deputy Chairmen, the Secretary, and 20 members. As in previous convocations, the members include a high proportion of important Party functionaries—14 of the 20 are full or candidate-members of the CPSU Central Committee and include Brezhnev, the Secretary-General of the CPSU, and three other full or candidate-members of the Politburo.

On his assumption of the Chairmanship of the Council of Ministers in March, 1958, Khrushchev was not re-elected to membership of the Presidium, by virtue of the fact that:

'in connection with the accountability of the Government to the

Presidium of the Supreme Soviet of the USSR, members of the Government cannot at the same time be members of the Presidium of the Supreme Soviet of the USSR.'[28]

While formally correct, this provision, in the wider context of the Soviet political system, is also an example of official hypocrisy. For there is nothing to prevent members of the Party Politburo, which actually frames policy, from being members of the Government. Khrushchev, after March, 1958, was First Secretary of the Central Committee of the CPSU, a member of its Presidium (now Politburo) and Chairman of the Council of Ministers of the USSR. The three most important members of the present Government, appointed in August, 1966, Kosygin, Chairman of the USSR Council of Ministers, and his two first deputies, Mazurov and Polyansky, are all members of the Party Politburo.

The Secretary of the Supreme Soviet Presidium is in general charge of the latter's secretariat; introduces edicts of the Presidium for confirmation by the Supreme Soviet and, together with the Chairman, countersigns such edicts and the laws and decrees of the Supreme Soviet itself. The post appears to be sufficiently important for it to have been considered expedient at the time of Stalin's death temporarily to replace its former occupant, A. F. Gorkin, by N. M. Pegov, at that time a Secretary of the Party Central Committee.

The proceedings of the Presidium are not made public, nor is there any indication of how frequently it meets, although it has been referred to as a 'daily working organ'.[29] More recently it has been stated that it meets 'periodically'.[30] Since, however, its members are drawn, for representative purposes, from widely dispersed areas and are, in any case, engaged in more demanding activities in their own localities (the deputy chairmen, for instance, are also the Chairmen of the Supreme Soviet Presidia of their own Republics) it is plainly impossible that the whole of the Presidium should sit regularly as a deliberative body. The 'daily working organ' is more likely a much smaller nucleus of available members, including the Chairman and the Secretary.

Under the Constitution (Article 48) the Presidium is declared to be accountable for all its activities to the Supreme Soviet, which has the power to elect a new Presidium at any time. The Presidium, as the 'collective' president of the USSR, does not, it is stated, possess the right of the French and American

Presidents to veto, delay or send back for reconsideration a statute adopted by the legislature, since once adopted by the Supreme Soviet of the USSR a statute becomes operative without further action.[31]

According to Article 49 of the USSR Constitution, which enumerates its powers and functions, the Presidium of the USSR Supreme Soviet:

(*a*) Convenes the sessions of the USSR Supreme Soviet;

(*b*) Issues edicts;

(*c*) Gives interpretations of the laws of the USSR in operation;

(*d*) Dissolves the USSR Supreme Soviet in conformity with Article 47 of the USSR Constitution and orders new elections;

(*e*) Conducts nation-wide polls (referenda) on its own initiative or on the demand of one of the Union Republics;

(*f*) Annuls decisions and orders of the USSR Council of Ministers and of the Councils of Ministers of the Union Republics if they do not conform to law;

(*g*) in the intervals between sessions of the USSR Supreme Soviet, releases and appoints Ministers of the USSR on the recommendation of the Chairman of the USSR Council of Ministers, subject to subsequent confirmation by the USSR Supreme Soviet;

(*h*) Institutes decorations (Orders and Medals) and titles of honour of the USSR;

(*i*) Awards Orders and Medals and confers titles of honour of the USSR;

(*j*) Exercises the right of pardon;

(*k*) Institutes military titles, diplomatic ranks and other special titles;

(*l*) Appoints and removes the High Command of the USSR Armed Forces;

(*m*) In the intervals between sessions of the USSR Supreme Soviet, proclaims a state of war in the event of military attack on the USSR, or when necessary to fulfil international treaty obligations concerning mutual defence against aggression;

(*n*) Orders general or partial mobilisation;

(*o*) Ratifies and denounces international treaties of the USSR;

(*p*) Appoints and recalls plenipotentiary representatives of the USSR to foreign States;

(*q*) Receives the letters of credence and recall of diplomatic representatives accredited to it by foreign States;

(*r*) Proclaims martial law in separate localities or throughout the USSR in the interests of the defence of the USSR or of the maintenance of public order and the security of the State.

Descriptions in Soviet sources of the competence of the Presidium emphasise that it does not issue laws (*Zakony*), said to be the unique prerogative of the Supreme Soviet, but merely interprets them, and issues edicts (*Ukazy*), which have less juridical importance than *Zakony*. Some, but not all, of its edicts have to be approved by the Supreme Soviet. Among those which must be approved are edicts which amend existing legislation and those concerning appointments and dismissals of Ministers.[32]

It is perhaps worth noting that before 1947 clauses 'b' and 'c' of Article 49 of the USSR Constitution were combined in a single clause. This read: '... gives interpretations of the laws of the USSR in operation, issues edicts', a version which could reasonably be taken to mean that edicts could only be issued for the purpose of clarifying existing statutes. The present clause 'b' leaves undefined the nature of the edicts which the Presidium may issue. The fact that these have frequently been tantamount to fresh legislation, and not merely based on existing statutes, has been demonstrated in an earlier section (see section on the 1936 Constitution).

The Presidium has never had occasion to dissolve the Supreme Soviet, in accordance with Article 47 of the Constitution, on account of disagreement between the Chambers, nor has it initiated or, as far as is known, been asked by a Union Republic to carry out a referendum. Its remaining prerogatives have been exercised at one time or another. Its main function has been to act as a continuously operating body at the summit of the Soviet structure, frequently serving as a legislative organ between sessions of the Supreme Soviet.

THE SUPREME SOVIETS OF THE REPUBLICS

The Soviet structure of the Union and Autonomous Republics is modelled on that of the USSR itself. The 15 Union Republics each have a Supreme Soviet of from 178 (Estonia) to 884 (RSFSR) members, which is unicameral even in the case of those Union Republics that contain Autonomous Republics. The latter have somewhat smaller single-chamber Supreme Soviets. Representation is related in both cases to population, and is set down in each Republic's Constitution.

The Supreme Soviet of each Republic is constitutionally conceived as the highest organ of State power in the Republic and as its sole legislative organ. It is elected by universal adult suffrage for four years, and the elections take place in the years following those to the USSR Supreme Soviet. The last elections to Republican Supreme Soviets were held in March, 1967.

The frequency of sessions of the Supreme Soviets of the Union and Autonomous Republics is prescribed in their respective Constitutions, although they all agree on the same minimum of two sessions a year. In practice, however, this Constitutional provision has often been violated. Thus, in 1956, it was reported that 'Not infrequently ... sessions of the Supreme Soviets, contrary to the requirements of the Constitution, are called only once a year'.[33] The Party group of a Republic Supreme Soviet, composed of deputies who are Party members, may hold a meeting in advance of a session 'for a preliminary examination of the questions to be raised.'[34]

The Supreme Soviets each elect a Chairman and a number of deputy chairmen to preside at sittings of the single-chamber legislature. Each Supreme Soviet also elects its Presidium, whose functions, *vis-à-vis* the Supreme Soviet and its organs, are analogous with those of the Presidium of the USSR Supreme Soviet, and a Government or Council of Ministers whose structure resembles that of the Federal Council of Ministers. In addition, the Union Republic Supreme Soviet elects permanent Commissions similar to those of the federal Supreme Soviet. It may also form such additional permanent Commissions as may be deemed necessary. Thus, in March, 1957, the RSFSR Supreme Soviet elected, in addition to the Mandate, Budget, Legislative Proposals and Foreign Affairs Commissions, four other permanent Commissions for Industry and Transport, Agriculture, Education and Culture, and Public Health and Social Insurance.[35]

The powers of the Supreme Soviet of a Union Republic are enumerated in Article 60 of the USSR Constitution, as follows:

The Supreme Soviet of a Union Republic:

(*a*) Adopts the Constitution of the Republic and amends it in conformity with Article 16 of the USSR Constitution. (This states that the Constitution of a Union Republic 'takes account of the specific features of the Republic and is drawn up in full conformity with the USSR Constitution');

(*b*) Confirms the Constitutions of the Autonomous Republics forming part of it and defines the boundaries of their territories;

(*c*) Approves the national-economic plan and the budget of the Republic;

(*d*) Exercises the right of amnesty and pardon of citizens sentenced by judicial organs of the Union Republic:

(e) Decides questions of representation of the Union Republic in its international relations;

(f) Determines the manner of organising the Republic's military formations.

As has already been indicated in the section on the Constitution, the last two paragraphs are in practice virtually inoperative. Only in the fields covered by para. (c) has there been a certain devolution of responsibility from the centre to the republics in recent years; but since, in practice, this concerns the Council of Ministers more than the Supreme Soviet itself, it is dealt with in the relevant section.

Since February, 1957, there has been some extension of the rights of the Union Republics in the sphere of legislation. At its session that month the USSR Supreme Soviet empowered Republican authorities to decide questions of the administrative and territorial division of their areas without reference to the All-Union authorities, provided that this did not affect the status of the Autonomous Republics and *oblasts* within the Union Republics, which remained the responsibility of the Central Government.[36] A further law passed at the same session gave the Union Republics the right to establish their own Criminal, Civil and Procedural Codes.[37]

Under this the definition of basic principles governing all criminal, civil and procedural law remains the responsibility of the All-Union authorities, while the Republics, once these principles are established, adapt them to the specific conditions and requirements prevailing in their own territories. It has been emphasised that there must be identical treatment in the codes of such features as the use of punishment, military offences, offences against property and others.[38]

This law restored the position which existed before 1936, when all Union Republics had their own codes, and reversed the decision taken at the 19th Party Congress in 1952 to draw up a single Criminal Code for the whole of the USSR.

Limited though the powers of the Union Republics clearly are, those of the so-called Autonomous Republics are even more exiguous. They have no constitutionally proclaimed right of secession, and para. b of Article 60 of the USSR Constitution makes it plain that they have no control over their own boundaries. Even their Constitutions require to be ratified by the Union Republic Supreme Soviets.

The powers of the Supreme Soviets of the Autonomous Re-

[69]

publics of the RSFSR are defined as follows in Article 59 of the RSFSR Constitution:

The Supreme Soviet of an Autonomous Republic:

(a) Adopts the Constitution of the Autonomous Republic and submits it for ratification by the RSFSR Supreme Soviet;

(b) Establishes the *raion* division of the Autonomous Republic and the boundaries of *raions* and towns and submits them for ratification by the RSFSR Supreme Soviet;

(c) Approves the national-economic plan and budget of the Autonomous Republic;

(d) Awards honorary titles of the Autonomous Republic.

The Autonomous Republic is fundamentally a ward of the Union Republic of which it forms part and which is responsible for its economic and cultural development.

Republican Supreme Soviets, no less than the USSR Supreme Soviet, function largely as rubber-stamp bodies, and their impotence is reflected in the apathy of their members, who appear to concern themselves with a minimum of business. Thus, one noted ideologist, writing in the Party's principal journal in 1956, complained that

'there are substantial defects in the work of the Supreme Soviets of the Republics. For instance . . . the Supreme Soviet of the Kazakh SSR, except for discussing the budgets and confirming the edicts of its Presidium, has not examined a single question relating to the economic and cultural life of the Republic and has never once heard the reports of the Ministries or of the local executive organs. Questions connected with the improvement of the work of the local Soviets are rarely discussed at the sessions of the Supreme Soviets of the Union and Autonomous Republics.'[39]

Even on the rare occasions when a Republican Supreme Soviet does discuss a matter of importance its discussions are empty formalities:

'At present, draft laws approving the economic plan and State budget and material relating to them are distributed to Deputies only just before the opening of the Supreme Soviet session at which they are to be examined. As a result, the Deputies are unable to prepare themselves adequately for the discussion of these matters, to consult in advance local organs of administration of their electors, or to collect the necessary information, etc. . . . obviously in this situation it is difficult for the majority of Deputies to get to the bottom of matters or take an active part in the discussion.'[40]

1. Stalin, *Problems of Leninism*, p. 708.
2. Kravtsov, *Verkhovny Sovet SSSR*, p. 40.
3. *Ibid.*, p. 42.
4. *Osnovy Sovetskogo Gosudarstvennogo Stroitelstva i Prava*, p. 210.
5. *Izvestiya*, December 5, 1965.
6. *B.S.E.*, 2nd edn., Vol. 35, p. 400.
7. *Pravda*, December 25, 1956.
8. *B.S.E.*, 2nd edn., Vol. 35, p. 400.
9. *Sovetskoe Gosudarstvo i Pravo*, No. 4, 1966, p. 35.
10. *Novikov*, p. 13.
11. *Ibid.*, pp. 9, 26.
12. *Sovetskoe Gosudarstvo i Pravo*, No. 4, 1966, p. 37.
13. Novikov, p. 26.
14. *Ibid.*, pp. 26, 33.
15. *Ibid.*, pp. 12, 27.
16. *e.g. Sovety Deputatov Trudyashchikhsya*, No. 6, 1958.
17. Kravtsov, *Sovetskaya Izbiratelnaya Sistema*, p. 35.
18. *Sovety Deputatov Trudyashchikhsya*, No. 2, 1958, pp. 7–8.
19. *Ibid.*, p. 5.
20. *Ibid.*
21. Lenin, *Sochineniya*, Vol. 25, p. 396.
22. Kravtsov, *Verkhovny Sovet SSSR*, p. 67.

23. Lenin, *Sochineniya*, Vol. 26, p. 301.
24. Filonovich, p. 19.
25. *Vedomosti Verkhovnogo Soveta SSSR*, No. 25, 1966; *USSR, Questions and Answers*, p. 50.
26. Stalin, *Problems of Leninism*, pp. 708–9.
27. *Osnovy Sovetskogo Gosudarstvennogo Stroitelstva i Prava*, pp. 226–7.
28. *B.S.E.*, 2nd edn., Vol. 50, p. 10.
29. Vyshinsky, p. 334.
30. *Osnovy Sovetskogo Gosudarstvennogo Stroitelstva i Prava*, p. 231.
31. Vyshinsky, pp. 331–2, *Osnovy Sovetskogo Gosudarstvennogo Stroitelstva i Prava*, p. 217.
32. Petrov, p. 113.
33. *Sovetskoe Gosudarstvo i Pravo*, No. 3, 1956, p. 6.
34. *Osnovy Sovetskogo Gosudarstvennogo Stroitelstva i Prava*, p. 235.
35. *Sovetskaya Rossiya*, March 15, 1957.
36. *Vedomosti Verkhovnogo Soveta SSSR*, No. 4, 1957.
37. *Ibid.*
38. *Pravda*, February 12, 1957.
39. *Kommunist*, No. 8, 1956 (article by Burlatski).
40. *Sovetskoe Gosudarstvo i Pravo*, No. 11, 1965, p. 14

V

The Councils of Ministers

The Federal Government of the Soviet Union is the USSR Council of Ministers, described in the Constitution as the 'highest executive and administrative organ of the State power of the USSR' (Article 64). It is stated to be 'responsible and accountable' to the Supreme Soviet or, between sessions of the latter, to its Presidium, which can annul its enactments if they do not conform to Statute Law (Articles 65, 49f). In consequence of the present Constitution's explicit provision that legislative power is vested in the Supreme Soviet alone, the Council of Ministers, it is repeatedly emphasised, does not exercise legislative power (as the Council of People's Commissars did under the 1924 Constitution) but functions exclusively as an executive-administrative body, whose task is to co-ordinate and direct the activity of the entire apparatus of State administration.

It has no discretionary powers in the sense of being able to operate outside the law or to modify or annul laws, and its legislative rôle is stated to be confined to the exercise of the right of legislative initiative.[1] In the performance of its duties it is empowered to issue decrees and ordinances 'binding throughout the territory of the USSR', and to verify their execution, but such enactments are issued only 'on the basis and in pursuance of laws in operation' (Articles 66, 67). The distinction between the two types of enactment of the Council of Ministers appears to be that whereas a decree 'is an act adopted in collegial fashion, after the appropriate discussion by members of the government ... as a rule having a normative character', ordinances 'are adopted by the Chairman of the government [*i.e.* the Council of Ministers] personally, or by his deputy, and concern questions which need a swift, practical decision, and which by their nature are unsuitable for wide collegial discussion ... for the most part ... they relate to individual facts or persons; they are of lesser importance compared to the government's decrees'.[2]

The functions of the USSR Council of Ministers are listed in Article 68 of the Constitution, as follows:

The USSR Council of Ministers:

(a) Co-ordinates and directs the work of the All-Union and Union-Republican Ministries of the USSR of the State Committees of the Council of Ministers of the USSR and of other institutions under its jurisdiction.

(b) Adopts measures to carry out the national-economic plan and the State Budget, and to strengthen the credit and monetary system;

(c) Adopts measures for the maintenance of public order, for the protection of the interests of the State, and for the safeguarding of the rights of citizens;

(d) Exercises general guidance in the sphere of relations with foreign states;

(e) Fixes the annual contingents of citizens to be called up for military service and directs the general organisation of the Armed Forces of the country;

(f) Sets up State Committees of the USSR, and, whenever necessary, special Committees and Chief Administrations under the Council of Ministers of the USSR for economic and cultural affairs and defence.

In addition, the USSR Council of Ministers has the right, in respect of those branches of administration and the economy placed within the competence of the USSR, to 'suspend decrees and ordinances of the Councils of Ministers of the Union Republics, and to annul orders and instructions of Ministers of the USSR and also the acts of other institutions under its jurisdiction' (Article 69).

COMPOSITION OF COUNCIL OF MINISTERS

The Council of Ministers is formed by the Supreme Soviet at the first session of a new convocation. In accordance with Article 70 of the Constitution, the outgoing Chairman of the Council of Ministers lays down its powers on the expiry of its term of office, *i.e.* when a new Supreme Soviet is elected. After formal approval of the work of the outgoing Council of Ministers, a proposal is put forward on the appointment of the new Chairman, who submits his Government for approval at the next joint sitting of the Chambers. Between sessions of the Supreme Soviet, individual Ministers are appointed and released, on the recommendation of the Chairman of the Council of Ministers, by the Presidium of the Supreme Soviet, with subsequent submission of such appointments for confirmation by the Supreme Soviet (Article 49g of the Constitution). Members of the Government are not required to be members of the Supreme Soviet.

The industrial administration reform of May, 1957, entailed a considerable transformation of the traditional structure pattern of the USSR Council of Ministers. The main changes were: the abolition of ten All-Union and 15 Union-Republican industrial ministries; the merging of a number of Ministries and the transformation of others into State Committees. A hierarchy of regional economic councils (*sovnarkhozy*) culminating in the Supreme Economic Council (VSNKh, established in March, 1963) was set up. The industrial State committees were subordinated to this latter body via *Gosplan, Gosstroi* (State Committee for Construction) and the USSR Economic Council, and it was supposed to take over from the USSR Council of Ministers many of the latter's functions with regard to administrating industry and construction. In practice, however, it never appears to have become fully operative.

The whole reform was unscrambled after Khrushchev's fall, and the traditional pattern was restored in October, 1965, when industrial Ministries were re-established in the place of State Committees. The size of the Council of Ministries was also then reduced by removing from it four Chairmen of non-industrial State Committees, and 16 officials (such as Deputy Chairmen of *Gosplan*) who were no longer accorded the personal rank of Minister.

On August 3, 1966, the USSR Council of Ministers consisted of a Chairman; two First Deputy Chairmen; nine Deputy Chairmen; 47 heads of All-Union and Union-Republican Ministries; seven Chairmen of State Committees and Committees; and 18 other members: the 15 Chairmen of Union Republic Councils of Ministers; the head of the Central Statistical Administration, and the Chairmen of the State Bank and the All-Union Farm Machinery Association. Total membership was thus 84. (It subsequently rose to 86, with the appointment of Ministers for Preservation of Public Order and Education.) All except one (the Chairman of the State Committee for the Timber Industry) were full or candidate-members of the CPSU Central Committee or members of its Revision Commission.

Whatever the theoretical distinctions between laws passed by the Supreme Soviet, edicts issued by its Presidium and decrees promulgated by the Council of Ministers, in practice it is the last-named which, by the scope and volume of its enactments, has been the principal source of legislation within the Soviet State system. The Council of Ministers has issued a multitude of decrees, rules and regulations governing virtually every aspect of economic and social life inside the country: industry, agriculture, transport, trade, education, social insurance, public health, etc. It also co-ordinates and supervises the organisation of the Armed Forces and national defence, and exercises over-all direction of the country's foreign policy and foreign trade.

It is a peculiarity of the Soviet system that, in internal affairs at any rate, it is frequently difficult to determine the division of competence between the State organ and those of the Party. At Government level their powers have appeared to coalesce, and the Council of Ministers and the Central Committee often operate jointly. Thus the more important economic decrees are usually issued in the names of both the Central Committee of the CPSU and the Council of Ministers. A recent example was a decree on land improvement in order to increase agricultural crops.[3] There is no specific constitutional provision for enactments of this kind, which are said to 'regulate the most important questions of economic and political life; in them a Party directive is merged with a State act'.[4]

Although Soviet writers insist that the acts of the Council of Ministers are inferior in standing to laws, *i.e.* to Statutes passed by the Supreme Soviet, it is also stated that they 'are not subject to control from the point of view of their legality by any organs other than higher organs of State power. The acts of the Government are obligatory for unconditional application by all, including the Courts'.[5] Only the Supreme Soviet and its Presidium have the theoretical power to annul the Government's acts—a power which has never been exercised. In practice, the Government's acts have the authority and the effect of law, and indeed, as was indicated earlier (see the section on the 1936 Constitution), there have been occasions when they have introduced material changes into the Constitution itself.

The authority of the Council of Ministers, however, has derived, not from its position in the State system (its constitutional powers being in theory merely administrative, are not very great) but from the standing in the Party hierarchy of its more important members and their consequent ability to transform it into a centre of power. While 'dual rule', as between the Government and Party bureaucracies is no doubt bound to create friction, under Stalin this did not manifest itself as obviously as it did subsequently, because he controlled both the Council of Ministers and Party Secretariat and also the instruments of coercion. It was after his death, when the Government bureaucracy and the Party machine, whose rights and obligations were not clearly distinguished, came under separate direction that the trend towards conflict became more apparent.

While Malenkov's enforced resignation from the Chairmanship of the Council of Ministers in February, 1955, betokened a weakening of the Government bureaucracy *vis-à-vis* the Party machine, nevertheless up to the middle of 1957 the Government was still a considerable centre of power, potentially capable of resisting inroads into its authority from the Party apparatus, by virtue of the fact that its most important members (the Chairman, five First Deputy Chairmen and one Deputy Chairman) constituted a putative majority in the Party Presidium, where State policy is determined. The notion that the Party should rule and the Government merely administer could not be applied in practice when the Government was controlled by such high-powered individuals. It is significant that one of the charges against the 'anti-Party group' of Malenkov, Molotov and Kaganovich by the Central Committee's ideological organ was that they 'departed from the Leninist concept of the leading rôle of the Communist Party', and certain of them were accused (though not by name) of advocating the 'primacy of State organs over those of the Party'.[5]

The measures taken against the 'anti-Party group' at the June, 1957, Plenum of the Central Committee immediately brought about changes in the Council of Ministers which deprived it of power and prestige. By the elimination of five Party Presidium members (Molotov, Kaganovich, Malenkov, Pervukhin and Saburov)—only Bulganin and Mikoyan remained—its political importance was destroyed.

The Government formed by Khrushchev after his assumption of the Chairmanship of the Council of Ministers in March, 1958, showed the extent to which the importance of that body had been reduced. In contrast to the practice of the Stalin era, when the economic planners—Kuibyshev, Mezhlauk, Ordzhonikidze and Voznesensky—were also members of the Polit-buro, the key economic posts were entrusted to technical experts with no voice in the higher Party councils. For almost two years (until March, 1959) the head of *Gosplan* was I. I. Kuzmin, who was not even a candidate-member of the Central Committee.[7] Much of the machinery of Central Government had already been atomised by the economic reorganisation of May, 1957 (over which the Government-Party conflict reached its crisis peak) which placed the management of industry and construction on a territorial, instead of the pre-vious highly centralised, functional basis. This reform was taken over directly by the Party Secretariat. The draft plan was put forward not by Bulganin, Chairman of the Council of Ministers, but by Khrushchev, First Secretary of the Party Central Committee; and it was not a State organ but the Bureau of the Central Committee for the RSFSR, of which Khrushchev was also chairman, that organised a conference of Chairmen of the newly-formed Councils of National Economy (Sovnarkhozy) of the RSFSR. Of the six leading participants mentioned in the press, only one, Bulganin, was a member of the Government: the rest were members of the Party Central Committee Secretariat.[8]

Thus even before the June, 1957, Plenum and the ousting of the 'anti-Party group', the Party Secretariat appeared to have wrested the initiative from the Government. What Khrushchev then did was to destroy completely the 'dual rule' of Party and Government by transposing the preponderance of Presidium representation from the Council of Ministers to the Party Secretariat and, in effect, reducing the Council of Ministers to the status of an administrative channel for direct Party rule.

Upon Khrushchev's removal in October, 1964, the Central Committee reportedly resolved that, to avoid a recurrence of one-man rule, the First Secretary of the Party should not again, except in a national emergency, also assume the Chairmanship of the Council of Ministers. A tacit agreement was apparently reached to preserve a balance between the Party and the Government, headed respectively by Brezhnev and Kosygin, though the supremacy of the Party was stressed, and unques-tioned precedence given to Brezhnev as its First Secretary. So far this arrangement seems to have worked satisfactorily.

[77]

In an interview with the managing editor of the *New York Times* in May, 1957, Khrushchev said that the USSR Council of Ministers met at least once a week.[9] It seems highly unlikely that the whole of the Council of Ministers, with a membership of 84, would meet as frequently as this. Moreover, with the inclusion of the 15 Chairmen of the Councils of Ministers of the Union Republics, geographical considerations make such frequent meetings physically improbable.

There can be little doubt that the effective Cabinet in the sense of a policy-making and deliberative body is the Presidium of the Council of Ministers. The existence of such an inner body, for which there is no constitutional provision, was revealed, together with that of the 'inner-inner' body called the Bureau of the Presidium of the Council of Ministers, in a joint decree of the Party Central Committee, the Council of Ministers and the Presidium of the Supreme Soviet published two days after Stalin's death.[10] The decree 'recognised the necessity of having in the USSR Council of Ministers, instead of two organs—the Presidium and the Bureau of the Presidium, a single organ—the Presidium of the USSR Council of Ministers', which was to consist of the Chairman and the First Deputy-Chairmen.

A pointer to the political importance of the Presidium of the Council of Ministers during the subsequent period was provided at the time of Malenkov's removal from the Premiership in February, 1955. Although he remained a member of the Party Presidium, he seems to have been debarred from simultaneous membership of the Presidium of the Council of Ministers by being demoted to Deputy Chairman. He was the only member of the Party Presidium in the Government who was not a *First* Deputy Chairman.

Just who is a member of the Presidium of the Council of Ministers at any given time is a matter of speculation. According to a legal textbook, it consists of the Chairman of the Council of Ministers, his first Deputies and Deputies, and 'officials personally appointed by the Council of Ministers'.[11]

ORGANS OF THE COUNCIL OF MINISTERS—THE
MINISTRIES

The Ministries of the USSR, which exist at Federal level, are of two kinds: All-Union and Union-Republican. The All-Union Ministries direct the branches of the administration entrusted to them throughout the territory of the USSR either directly or through organs appointed by them; the Union-Republican Ministries do so, as a rule, through Ministries of the same name in some or all of the Union-Republics, administering directly only a limited number of enterprises according to a list confirmed by the Presidium of the USSR Supreme Soviet (Articles 75, 76 of the Constitution).

Before the industrial reorganisation of May, 1957, economic Ministries managed as well as supervised the enterprises coming under their jurisdiction. The point of the reorganisation was to break up the ministerial empires which had grown up under Stalin, and improve co-operation between enterprises in the same region. Direct administration was entrusted to the local *Sovnarkhozy*, while in Moscow, the State Committees which replaced the Ministries were supposed to have no direct administrative responsibilities. The new system, however, gave rise to new distortions of the economy as vexing as those it was intended to overcome (especially 'localism' or 'parochialism') which Khrushchev attempted to combat by re-centralisation, e.g., by establishing Republican and then an All-Union *Sovnarkhoz* to co-ordinate the local *sovnarkhozes*. The post-Khrushchev leadership, after some initial hesitation, decided to abandon the *Sovnarkhoz* system and revert to industrial Ministries. But official spokesmen have repeatedly stressed that the re-establishment of these Ministries 'does not mean a simple return to the structure of industrial administration operating prior to 1957'. Mazurov, who reported on this subject to the USSR Supreme Soviet in October, 1965, declared:

'The newly organised Ministries will work in a situation where the rights of enterprises are considerably widened and their economic independence increased. Therefore the Ministries must know how to combine economic methods with the carrying out of their administrative functions . . . and must renounce the petty tutelage of enterprises which was characteristic of the former Ministries.'

The structural organisation of the Ministries appears to be much as it was prior to 1957, and is defined in an instrument (*polozhenie*) approved for each Ministry by the Council of Ministers. In each Ministry, in addition to the Minister, there are usually a number of Deputy Ministers in charge of the several main divisions. Like many of the Ministers themselves, these men are, in the majority of cases, technical specialists rather than politicians. They are appointed and dismissed by the Council of Ministers, on the representation of the Minister. The organisational basis of a Ministry's activity is stated to be the principle of 'one-man management' (edinonachalie), i.e., personal responsibility of the Minister for the whole activity of his department.[12] This does not, however, preclude collectivity of discussion within the Ministry, and for this purpose a deliberative and advisory organ or collegium (kollegia) is set up under the Minister's chairmanship, consisting of the Deputy Ministers and leading officials of the Ministry, which is confirmed by the Council of Ministers on the Minister's representation [13] The collegium is conceived to have an important part to play in keeping watch on what is going on at lower levels and in checking on the performance of the Ministry's own departments. For this purpose it may demand reports from administration and departmental heads and from the heads of organisations and enterprises under the ministry's jurisdiction. In the case of a Union-Republican Ministry its collegium also has the right to hear reports from the corresponding ministry in the Union Republic. The collegium participates in drafting and discussion of the more important of the ministry's juridical acts and in the selection of personnel. It also considers new working methods and techniques and ways of promoting 'Socialist competition'.[14]

Since the Minister is held personally responsible for the work of the Ministry, it follows that his decision must prevail in the event of disagreement. The instruments regulating the work of ministries provide that if there is a divergence of opinion between the Minister and the collegium the Minister takes his own decision, at the same time bringing any disagreement that has arisen to the notice of the Council of Ministers, to which members of the collegium also have the right of appeal.[15]

The two types of act which a Minister is constitutionally empowered to promulgate are known as orders (prikazy) and instructions (instruktsii). These he may issue, within the limits of his Ministry's jurisdiction, only on the basis and in pursuance of the operative laws and also of the decrees and ordinances of the Council of Ministers (Article 73). The distinction between an instruction and an order appears to be that whereas the former is invariably of a general character, i.e., binding on all, the latter is usually addressed to a particular quarter. An instruction usually prescribes rules, indicating *how* a higher juridical act (law or Government ordinance) is to be applied; an order, on the other hand, envisages concrete application of the rules.

THE COUNCILS OF MINISTERS OF THE REPUBLICS

The Constitutions of all 15 Union Republics present an almost identical structure for their Councils of Ministers. Provision is made for a Chairman; First Deputy Chairmen; Deputy Chairmen; Ministers; and the Chairmen of State Committees (*e.g.*, for Planning, and for State Security), and the heads of bodies such as the Statistical Administration and the Administration for Material-Technical Supplies.

The powers of a Union Republic Council of Ministers, as defined in the USSR Constitution, are closely modelled on those of the All-Union Government, but are confined to the territory of the Republic. Like its Federal counterpart, it is empowered to issue and verify the execution of decrees and ordinances, but these must be based on, and in pursuance of, not only the laws of the Union Republic itself but also the laws of the USSR and the decrees and ordinances of the USSR Council of Ministers (Article 81). Apart from directing and co-ordinating the work of their own Ministries and institutions under their immediate jurisdiction, a major task of the Union Republic Councils of Ministers appears to be the direction of the work of Councils of Ministers of Autonomous Republics and of Executive Committees of *krai* and *oblast* Soviets—or of *raion* Soviets if the Republic has no *oblast* division—and the systematic consideration of reports from them, which are 'as a rule, accompanied by co-reports of persons who on instructions from the Council of Ministers have previously examined the activity of the Executive Committee concerned'.[16] Union Republican Councils of Ministers have the right to annul the acts of Ministries and Executive Committees of local soviets and to suspend those of Councils of Ministers of Autonomous Republics and of local soviets (RSFSR Constitution, Article 46). The powers of Republic Ministries themselves are similarly defined in the same terms as those of the corresponding bodies at All-Union level, with the additional proviso, stemming again from the unitary concept of democratic centralism, that their acts must be in conformity with those of the corresponding Union-Republican Ministries at the Centre (RSFSR Constitution, Article 50).

Being at one further remove down the vertical line of subordination, the Councils of Ministers and the Ministries of the Autonomous Republics must ensure that their acts are in conformity also with those of the Union Republic Council of Ministers and the Union Republic Ministries respectively (RSFSR Constitution, Articles 67 and 71).

In the Union Republics Ministries are of two kinds—Union-Republican and Republican. The difference between them lies in the fact that, whereas Republican Ministries are under the direct jurisdiction only of the Council of Ministers of the Union Republic, Union-Republican Ministries are under the simultaneous jurisdiction both of the Union Republic Council of Ministers and of the corresponding Union Republican Ministries at All-Union level.

Ministries in Autonomous Republics are not divided into categories but are all subordinate to corresponding Ministries at the level of the Union Republic, which may be of the Union-Republican or Republican type.

One of the major Soviet propaganda themes has been the extension of the rights of the Union Republics in economic and cultural matters and in legislation. During 1954 and 1955 a number of All-Union ministries were transformed into Union-Republican Ministries and thousands of enterprises transferred from All-Union jurisdiction to the corresponding ministries of the Union Republics. As a result production controlled by Republican and Union-Republican ministries in proportion to the gross industrial production of each Republic had increased by the beginning of 1956 to 70 per cent in the Ukraine, 71 per cent in Byelorussia, 74 per cent in Estonia, 78 per cent in Latvia, 79 per cent in Uzbekistan, 81 per cent in Azerbaidzhan, 92 per cent in Tadzhikistan and 62 per cent in Kazakhstan.[17]

The policy of 'bringing management closer to industrial undertakings' was endorsed by the 20th Congress of the CPSU in February, 1956. In the resolution on the report of the Central Committee it was proclaimed that 'the Ministries of the various Union Republics should be allowed still broader powers in the day-to-day management of industry, while the USSR Ministries retain general direction, determine plan assignments, supervise their fulfilment, direct the supply of equipment and the financing of capital investment.'[18] Clearly this policy was not primarily a concession to national sentiment, but part and parcel of an efficiency drive against which the excessive centralisation of the past had militated to a very dangerous degree. Nevertheless the advantages for the inhabitants of a Republic of Ministries of the Union-Republican over those of All-Union type can be real ones. Before the Ministry of Communications was changed from an All-Union to a Union-Republican type in 1955,[19] for example, it was difficult for local officials to complain to distant Moscow about the arbitrary action of men from the Ministry in cutting down prized boulevard trees to make way for telephone wires. When there is a responsible Minister sitting in the Republic's own Council of Ministers he is more readily accessible to complaints.

By the end of 1956 the Republic authorities had been empowered to plan the production and distribution of all types of goods produced by undertakings of local Republican industries, to determine the allocation of scarce goods between local enterprises and to utilise a large part of any production over and above the plan by undertakings under All-Union and Union-Republican control. The effect of these concessions on the economies of the Republics was described by Myurisep, Chairman of the Estonian Council of Ministers, in an article in the USSR Government newspaper:

'Formerly the national-economic plan of the Republic was determined to the smallest detail by the USSR *Gosplan*, which often did not take our special requirements into account. . . . From year to year local industry in Estonia was automatically allotted a plan to produce nails by the ton by the USSR *Gosplan*. To fulfil the plan the metal processing factories produced large nails although there was no demand for them. Small nails were therefore scarce everywhere. After the Republic was allowed to plan the assortment of products of local industries itself we quickly removed this shortage.'[20]

In the interests of efficiency the rights of the Union Republics in finance were also extended. In 1955 the Republican Councils of Ministers were granted the right to use extra allocations from Republican Budgets for financing housing and communal construction in excess of plan. Since 1955 they have also been empowered to distribute the revenue assigned to the Union Republics in the USSR State Budget as between the Republican and local budgets. Previously this had been determined for them by the USSR budget.

[83]

By the 'Law on the Further Improvement of Management in Industry and Construction in the USSR' passed by the USSR Supreme Soviet in May, 1957,[21] the devolution of administrative powers to the Union Republics was carried a stage further. The regional economic councils (*Sovnarkhozy*) which after July 1, 1957, assumed the functions of the majority of the former economic Ministries and to which all industrial undertakings, with few exceptions, were subordinated, were under the direct control of the Councils of Ministers of the Union Republics. The Chairmen of the Republican Councils of Ministers are *ex officio* members of the USSR Council of Ministers, and the central direction of the various economies is carried out through the relevant Republican Councils of Ministers.

At the September, 1965, Plenum of the CPSU Central Committee, at which Kosygin presented the plan for the reform of industrial administration, he said that:

'The Central Committee of the CPSU and the USSR Council of Ministers have discussed and adopted decisions to grant Union Republics additional rights in the fields of planning, capital construction, finance, labour and wages.'

When, over a year later, a decree on this subject was finally published, the 'additional rights' it granted the republics were of little or no significance.[22]

SOURCES

1. Askerov *et al.*, p. 394.
2. *Osnovy Sovetskogo Gosudarstvennogo Stroitelstva i Prava*, p. 254.
3. *Pravda*, June 19, 1966.
4. Askerov *et al.*, p. 396.
5. *Ibid.*, pp. 395–6.
6. *Kommunist*, No. 10, 1957, p. 5.
7. *Pravda*, March 21, 1959.
8. *Pravda*, June 2, 1957.
9. *Pravda*, May 14, 1957.
10. *Pravda*, March 7, 1953.
11. *Osnovy Sovetskogo Gosudarstvennogo Stroitelstva i Prava*, p. 251.
12. Ananov, p. 154.
13. Yampolskaya, p. 197.
14. *Ibid.*, p. 198.
15. Ananov, p. 160.
16. Yampolskaya, p. 208.
17. *Planovoe Khozyaistvo*, No. 4, 1956; *Pravda*, February 15, 1956.
18. *New Times*, No. 10, March 1, 1956.
19. *Vedomosti Verkhovnogo Soveta SSSR*, No. 1, 1955.
20. *Izvestiya*, September 22, 1956.
21. *Vedomosti Verkhovnogo Soveta SSSR*, No. 11, 1957.
22. *Spravochnik Partiinogo Rabotnika*, p. 417.

VI

The Local Soviets

Local Soviets are those 'organs of State power' which exist at the various administrative levels below that of the republic— *krai, oblast*, autonomous *oblast*, national *okrug, raion*, city, rural locality (*stanitsa*, village, hamlet, *kishlak, aul*), city-*raion* and settlement. Under the USSR Constitution such local Soviets are elected by universal adult suffrage of the inhabitants of the respective localities for a period of two years (Article 95). At the 1965 elections there were 47,736 local Soviets with a total membership of over two million.

Within the Soviets are Party groups composed of all the deputies who are Party members. The groups are headed by a secretary and take their orders from the local Party Committee. Their principal task is to ensure that the Soviets carry out Party policy.[1]

The frequency of meetings of local Soviets is laid down in the Republics' Constitutions, but to judge by the constant criticism in the Soviet Press over the past years, many local Soviets have consistently failed to hold their sessions as regularly as they should. The Constitutions of the majority of the Union Republics stipulate that *krai* and *oblast* Soviets should meet not less than four times a year; city, *raion*, and village Soviets not less than six times a year, and Soviets of large cities, with *raion* division not less than four times a year. It was pointed out in 1956,[2] however, that in the previous year in the RSFSR there had been failure to call regular sessions of the Soviets in all cities of Republic subordination, in 66·6 per cent of the *okrugs*, in 40·3 per cent of the settlements and 36·5 per cent of the village Soviets. In the same year no sessions of the Krasnoyarsk and Khabarovsk *krai* Soviets and of the Amur, Gorky, Kaliningrad and Smolensk *oblast* Soviets were held for over five months.

Such practice was condemned by Voroshilov at the 20th Party Congress as detrimental to the 'principles of Soviet democratism' in that the Soviets failed to control and direct the executive organs accountable to them.[3] In this respect it may perhaps be regarded as a weakness of the system that it is precisely the executive organs which are constitutionally required to convene the sessions (RSFSR Constitution, Articles 84, 85, 86). More recently it was stated that in the Byelorussian SSR certain executive Committees of local Soviets fail to convene sessions for a long period and then, in an attempt to compensate for the omission, hold several sessions in quick succession. Frequently, sessions are held in the absence of a large part of the membership, and even, on occasion, without a quorum.[4] Meetings of local Soviets are presided over and directed by a Chairman and a Secretary, elected for the purpose at each separate session (RSFSR Constitution, Article 87).

EXECUTIVE COMMITTEES

The executive and administrative organ of a local Soviet is the Executive Committee which it elects, consisting of a Chairman, Deputy Chairmen, Secretary and members (USSR Constitution, Article 99). In small localities it consists of a Chairman, a single Deputy Chairman and a Secretary (Article 100). 'In large towns an inner body, the Presidium, may be formed out of the Chairman, his Deputies and the Secretary.'[5] The Executive Committee is directly accountable both to the Soviet which elected it and also to the Executive Committee of the next higher Soviet (Article 101). In practice it is found that the vertical line of subordination, leading eventually through the Executive Committees of higher Soviets and Republican Ministries to the USSR Council of Ministers, is of greater importance and effectiveness than the horizontal line of subordination to the local Soviet. There is abundant evidence that in many localities the Soviets exert little influence or control over their Executive Committees, whereas Executive Committees themselves frequently exercise their constitutional right to annul the acts of Executive Committees at lower levels and to suspend the acts of lower Soviets (RSFSR Constitution, Article 90).

Local Soviets are required to form departments and administrations under their Executive Committees, certain of which are obligatory and others which may be necessitated by the particular conditions of the territorial unit. Thus, in the RSFSR *krai* and *oblast* Soviets are, under Article 92 of the Constitution, required to set up:

Departments for	Administrations for
Public Health	Services to the Population
Communal Economy	Culture
Popular Education	Local Industry
General Affairs	Meat and Milk Industry
Organisational Instructors	Preservation of Public Order
Building and Architecture	Food Industry
Social Security	Building and Repair of Roads
Finance	Building Materials Industry
	Agriculture
	Fuel Industry
	Trade

With the approval of the Republic Council of Ministers, other departments and administrations may be formed appropriate to the local economy. In addition they all have a planning commission.

For *raions* and cities the Constitution does not require the forming of administrations but prescribes a list of departments —usually understood in Soviet terminology to be smaller units than administrations—covering most of the same branches of activity. For *raion* Executive Committees the *oblast* Soviet may, if circumstances warrant, authorise additional departments for communal economy, local industry and trade. City Soviets may also, depending on the city's economy, set up departments for local industry. (RSFSR Constitution, Articles 96, 99.) In the case of the Moscow City Soviet, in view of its increased links with foreign towns, an External Affairs Department of the Executive Committee has been formed.[6] Following the decree on housing construction at the end of July, 1957, which made Executive Committees responsible for ordering the construction of housing, cultural establishments and municipal and public facilities, many city Soviets have set up departments or administrations for capital construction under their Executive Committees.[7] Since the end of 1956 the internal affairs administrations and the militia administrations in *krais* and *oblasts* (which previously had been attached to the Executive Committees, but not even nominally under their control) have been reorganised into single Administrations for the preservation of public order of the Executive Committees of *krai* and *oblast* Soviets, while Militia departments in cities and *raions* have been reorganised into Militia Departments of the Executive Committees of city and *raion* Soviets.[8]

[87]

Like all other locally-appointed organs, departments and administrations are, in accordance with the principle of 'democratic centralism', subject to 'dual subordination'. This means that they are directly subordinate, horizontally, to their Soviet and its Executive Committee and, vertically, to the corresponding departments and administrations at the next higher territorial level.

Since the Soviet meets only periodically in full session the day-to-day administration of a locality is carried on by the Executive Committee and its subordinate organs, and Press accounts of local affairs contain far more references to the Executive Committee than to the theoretically more important organ which elected it. As at the higher levels of the State system, authority lies in practice with the Executive rather than with the representative branch of government. Formally the election of the Executive Committee, including the designation of its Chairman, Deputy Chairmen and Secretary, requires a vote of the Soviet itself, but in fact the Chairman is appointed by the Party Committee at the next higher level (*i.e.* the Chairman of a *raion* Executive Committee is designated by the *oblast* Party Committee), and the Deputy Chairmen and Secretary by the Party Committee at the Soviets' own territorial level. No case is recorded of a Soviet disputing or voting against such appointments.

Moreover, hundreds of instances have been reported of people occupying executive office in local Soviets of which they were not even deputies. At the beginning of 1956, for example, it was stated in the principal Soviet legal journal,[9] 2,025 people who were not deputies were working as Chairmen, Deputy Chairmen and Secretaries of Executive Committees of local Soviets in the RSFSR—534 of them as Chairmen. In 1954 in the Ukraine, 1,411 Chairmen of local Soviet Executive Committees (10·6 per cent of the total), and 1,643 Secretaries (12·3 per cent of the total) were not deputies. Similar instances were reported in Lithuania in 1965.[10] Such appointments are plainly illegal. The failure of the Party to ensure prior election to the Soviets of those concerned may have been due to lack of time or more probably reflects a realistic indifference to mere constitutional niceties, such as is expressed in the frequent failure to hold by-elections to fill vacancies in local Soviets.[11] There is thus more than an element of disingenuousness in the official deprecation of such practices, which are attributed to submissiveness on the part of the Soviets but which are also more often than not the direct result of the Party's disruption of democratic procedures.

It is perhaps not surprising, in view of the indifference and passivity of the Soviets and the feeling of protection the Chairmen of Executive Committees must derive from Party sponsorship, that the failure of Executive Committees to report to and consult their Soviets has become a nation-wide phenomenon. At the beginning of 1957 the central Party newspaper was able to state, a year after Voroshilov's strictures on the practice at the 20th Party Congress, that 'many Executive Committees and the heads of their administrations and departments . . . fail to account for their work to the Soviets'.[12] Since then there has been little or no improvement. Seventeen per cent of Executive Committees in Turkmenia and Kirgizia failed to report to their Soviets in 1963.[13] Several Executive Committees in Lithuania, including that of the Vilnius city soviet, failed to report in 1965.[14] Only 15 out of 55 *krai* or *oblast* Executive Committees in the RSFSR reported after the March, 1965, local elections.[15]

The Executive Committee is officially declared to be a collective, deliberative organ. But genuine collectivity rarely makes for speed in reaching decisions, and to obviate the 'negative aspects of this method of leadership', it is suggested, on the authority of Lenin, that collective discussion 'be reduced to a minimum'. Thus, one authority commends the example of the Executive Committees of the Moscow and Leningrad city Soviets, where there had been set up, 'narrowly collegial organs, the bureau of the Executive Committee, consisting of the Chairman of the Executive Committee, his Deputy-Chairmen and the Secretary. Without replacing the Executive Committee as a whole the bureau settles urgent questions. . .'.[16]

This tendency towards the formation of inner executive bodies, over which the representative body exercises little control, is a characteristic feature of the Soviet political system. At the beginning of 1957 a Central Committee decree drew attention to the fact that 'in many cases sessions of Soviets are confined to the discussion of minor questions of a current nature . . . and sometimes are held only for going through the form of approving draft decisions prepared by

[89]

the Executive Committees'.[17] Later on, the decree warns against 'permitting Executive Committees to replace Soviets in deciding questions which should be considered at sessions' and also against the 'practice of co-opting people for elective posts in the Soviets and dismissing Soviet workers without a decision of the Soviets'. 'According to the existing system', complained a Soviet legal authority, 'the Executive Committees can decide all questions assigned by the Statutes to the Soviets'. He went on:

'In this fashion, the range of questions considered at sessions [of the Soviets] is restricted and conditions are created for the supplanting of the Soviets by the Executive Committees.'[18]

PERMANENT COMMISSIONS

As in the Supreme Soviets, much of the preparatory work of local Soviets is done by the permanent Commissions they elect from among their members. There are nearly 300,000 Commissions consisting of 1·6 million Deputies (81·5 per cent of all Deputies).[19] The Commissions are set up in Soviets at all levels and consist of a Chairman and Secretary (plus a Deputy Chairman if they are large enough) and members. The largest Soviets (*oblasts* and large cities) may have up to 15 or more such bodies, *raion* Soviets and those of smaller towns may have seven to 10, and village Soviets three or four.[20] The Permanent Commissions may vary considerably according to the economy and circumstances of the area, but the commonest types are for the budget, agriculture, trade and different classes of industry, and for social services like education, health, communal economy, and social insurance.

Apart from deputies, Permanent Commissions make extensive use of the services of activists, of whom 2½ millions are said to participate in their work.[21] Whereas the deputy who is a member of a Permanent Commission has a decisive vote, the non-deputy activist has only a consultative voice. The practical disadvantage of this cannot be very great, however, since the Permanent Commission has no independent executive power and can only make proposals, which the Executive Committee may or may not endorse.[22] Nevertheless, it is officially recommended that the Permanent Commissions should be consulted by the Executive Committee when matters concerning their sphere of activity are under consideration.[23] If a Permanent Commission's proposals are rejected by the Executive it has the right in theory to raise the matter for discussion in the Soviets.[24]

The main value for the authorities of Permanent Commissions in local Soviets appears to be twofold: they are useful for creating among wide sections of the public a sense of participation in the running of the State, and thus surrounding the organs of authority with a measure of public support, and, perhaps even more important, they provide yet another mechanism for checking reaction in the localities to directives from higher levels. 'Permanent Commissions are most important assistants of the local Soviets in exercising control over the carrying out of resolutions of higher organs. . .'.[25] They are empowered to inspect enterprises and institutions, and their 'signals' are no doubt a valuable source of information on local conditions and moods.

THE FUNCTIONS OF LOCAL SOVIETS

The claim of Soviet propagandists that the system of elected Soviets at all administrative levels is the mainstay of political life in the USSR and an expression of true democracy is virtually meaningless as long as in practice the local Soviets have no real power whatsoever. The Soviet State system is a unitary one which admits of no distinction between central and local government, and the local Soviets, far from being the country's 'political foundation' (Article 2 of the Constitution), are merely the executors of policies dictated from above.

The functions of local Soviets are laid down in the USSR and Republic Constitutions only in the most general terms. Thus, in the RSFSR they 'direct cultural, political and economic construction in their territory, draw up the local budget, direct the activity of organs of administration subordinate to them, ensure preservation of State order, assist the strengthening of the country's defence-capacity, ensure the observance of laws and the protection of the rights of citizens' (Article 79). The Soviets of *krais, oblasts,* autonomous *oblasts* and *okrugs* also elect the courts of their respective areas for a term of five years (Article 112). For a number of years recurrent demands have appeared in the Soviet Press for new Statutes, to replace those adopted in the early 1930s, detailing the rights and duties of the different Soviets: lack of them has led to confusion and conflict between the various levels of local authorities.[26] At the end of 1957 the Presidium of the RSFSR Supreme Soviet endorsed a new Statute for the village Soviet in the RSFSR,[27] but the rights and obligation of the higher Soviets still remain inadequately defined.

The work of local Soviet Executive Committees is varied and complex, with the emphasis on economic and financial tasks. The work of Executive Committees of city Soviets betrays the same preoccupation with economic questions.

One of the emphasised functions of the local Soviet Executive Committee, arising from the concept of 'democratic centralism', is the supervision and direction of the work of their counterparts at lower levels. One of the recommended methods of such direction is the submission of work plans to higher Executive Committees. But 'guidance' can be taken too far: certain Executive Committees are criticised for burdening the agendas of lower Executive Committees by making them discuss at their meetings the latest decisions adopted by the former, and *raion* Executive Committees, which are applauded for giving 'guidance on matters of preparing and conducting sessions' of village Soviets, are warned against actually planning the sessions, since this is the constitutional responsibility of the Chairman of the village Soviet. Here is a fine distinction which is probably disregarded in practice.

Much of the day-to-day business of an Executive Committee is routine office work such as could be performed by officials and does not seem to require an elected body. The Secretary of the town Executive Committee of Millerovo (Kamensk *oblast*) complained in 1954,[28] during one of the periodic campaigns against bureaucracy and excessive paper-work in the State system, that during the first eight months of that year the Executive Committee had issued to citizens 6,000 certificates of various kinds, 4,000 entitlement booklets for the receipt of State assistance, more than 3,000 forms for the exchange of [internal] passports and 3,000 certificates for the receipt of fuel books to railway personnel. He suggested that the number of such documents could be reduced by a half or two-thirds. Nevertheless, it may be that it is precisely in this necessary routine office work that the authorities find the main practical value and justification of the Soviets and their Executive Committees.

Recently, however, there has been evidence that the practice of employing elected officials on work of a specialised legal nature in the Soviets may need to be reconsidered. It has been pointed out, for example, that of 112 Secretaries of *raion* and city Executive Committees in Azerbaidzhan, only two have had legal education, and this is given as one of the reasons why Executive Committees have, in a number of cases, issued acts contrary to existing legislation. In 1957 organs of the procuracy alone are said to have protested against about 150 such acts. Since the Secretary of an Executive Committee is in charge of formalising legal documents, it is argued he should be a specialist in constitutional and administrative law.[29]

Executive Committees should in most cases meet at least twice a month.[30] Some Executive Committees are criticised for meeting too frequently. The Executive Committee meets in private and its proceedings are not published. Not infrequently, however, criticisms appear in the Press which suggest that, while debate is freer in the Executive Committee than in the Soviet, it is not always effective in counteracting the arbitrariness of some Chairmen. For, in the paradoxical fashion of the Soviet system, although the Chairman of an Executive Committee lays himself open to censure by higher authority if he does not take sufficient account of the views of his colleagues, he must always be aware of the greater danger that he will be held personally responsible, at the risk of his career, for failure to complete plans on time. The twin concepts of collective consultation (*kollegialnost*) and one-man management (*edinonachalie*) are not easily reconciled.

SOURCES

1. Petrov, p. 161.

2. *Sovetskoe Gosudarstvo i Pravo*, No. 3, 1956, p. 8.

3. *Pravda*, February 21, 1956.

4. *Kommunist*, No. 13, 1958, p. 31.

5. Petrov, p. 156.

6. *Byulleten Ispolnitelnogo Komiteta Moskovskogo Gorodskogo Soveta Deputatov Trudyashchikhsya*, No. 11, 1958.

7. *Sovety Deputatov Trudyashchikhsya*, No. 9, 1958, p. 4.

8. *Partiinaya Zhizn*, No. 4, 1957, p. 67.

9. *Sovetskoe Gosudarstvo i Pravo*, No. 3, 1956, p. 9.

10. *Sovetskaya Litva*, March 1, 1966.

11. *Sovetskoe Gosudarstvo i Pravo*, No. 3, 1956, p. 5; *Sovety Deputatov Trudyashchikhsya*, No. 1, 1958, p. 96.

12. *Pravda,* January 24, 1957.
13. *Sovetskoe Gosudarstvo i Pravo,* No. 3, 1965, p. 13.
14. *Sovetskaya Litva,* March 1, 1966.
15. *Vedomosti Verkhovnogo Soveta RSFSR,* No. 45, 1966.
16. *Sovetskoe Gosudarstvo i Pravo,* No. 6, 1955, p. 11.
17. Malin *et al.,* p. 448.
18. *Sovetskoe Gosudarstvo i Pravo,* 1965, No. 4, p. 24.
19. *Kommunist,* 1966, No. 8, p. 82.
20. Luzhin, *Postoyannye Komissii Mestnykh Sovetov Deputatov Trudyashchikhsya,* p. 45.
21. *Kommunist,* No. 8, 1966, p. 82.
22. Luzhin, *op. cit.,* p. 49.

23. *Ibid.,* p. 53.
24. *Ibid.,* p. 51.
25. *Ibid.,* p. 40.
26. *Sovetskoe Gosudarstvo i Pravo,* No. 3, 1956, p. 15; *Izvestiya,* October 3, 1956; *Sovety Deputatov Trudyashchikhsya,* No. 10, 1958, p. 20; *Sovestskoe Gosudarstvo i Pravo,* 1965, No. 4, p. 20, *Izvestiya,* January 7, 1966.
27. *Vedomosti Verkhovnogo Soveta RSFSR,* No. 1, 1957.
28. *Izvestiya,* October 6, 1954.
29. *Bakinsky Rabochii,* August 6, 1958 (article by Aliev and others).
30. *Osnovy Sovetskogo Gosudarstvennogo Prava i Stroitelstva,* p. 312.

VII

The Communist Party

The study of a country's political system means the study of its methods and instruments of government. In the case of a democracy, such a study can be more or less confined to an examination of those institutions traditionally accepted as keys to the nature of a political system—elections, the legislature, the head of State, central and local government, etc.—through which the delegated power of the people is exercised. As has been seen, such institutions exist in the Soviet Union, but despite their complexity and the overlay of democratic trappings their political significance is slight. The key to the Soviet political system is the leadership group—the 'ruling party'— which is not answerable to the formally elected parliament and for which the vast State machine represents merely an administrative channel.

ORIGIN AND PRINCIPLES

At its Second Congress in 1903 the Russian Social Democratic Workers' Party (the party of Russian Marxists) split into two main factions. Not the least important issue was the question of the obligations of Party membership. Whereas Martov, who was to become leader of the Menshevik faction, advocated a broad-based party open to anyone who subscribed to its programme and was willing to work under its direction (while retaining the right to think and influence party policy), Lenin envisaged a narrow, closed body of dedicated, disciplined revolutionaries, strictly subordinate to centralised direction and operating as the militant vanguard of the working masses. By a series of 'accidents' such as the withdrawal of the Jewish *Bund* delegates, Lenin's caucus formed a majority at the close of the Congress and became known as the Bolshevik (majority) faction of the Russian Social Democratic Workers' Party until, on Lenin's motion, its name was changed to the Russian Communist Party (Bolsheviks) at the Seventh Party Congress of the Bolsheviks in March, 1918. Subsequently, on the formation of the Soviet Union, its name was changed to the All-Union Communist Party (Bolsheviks), and at the 19th Congress in 1952 the designation 'Bolsheviks' was dropped as being no longer necessary for the Party's identification, and its present title 'Communist Party of the Soviet Union' adopted.

The Party has continued to reflect Lenin's original conception of it as a monolithic and totalitarian party, a dedicated and hardened *élite* with a tradition of highly centralised leadership, uncompromising discipline and the subordination of means to ends. Centralism and unity were further consolidated by the Resolution on Party Unity,[1] drafted by Lenin himself and adopted at the Party's Tenth Congress in 1921, which demanded the 'complete annihilation of any fractionalism' and thus marked the beginning of the end of real freedom of discussion within the Party by creating an authoritative precedent on the basis of which any opposition to Party policy was liable in future to be construed as treason.

After the formation of the Russian Federation (RSFSR), in which the Ukraine, Latvia, Lithuania and Byelorussia became constituent Soviet republics, the Eighth Congress of the RKP (b), held in 1919, was quick to decree that the recognition of these separate republics did not in any way imply that the RKP should be reorganised on a federal basis; what was required was a 'single centralised Communist Party with a single Central Committee, directing the whole of the Party's work in all parts of the RSFSR. ... The Central Committees of the Ukrainian, Latvian, Lithuanian Communists enjoy the rights of *oblast* Committees of the Party and are wholly subordinate to the Central Committee of the RKP'.[2] Earlier there had been clear evidence that such a solution was regarded with apprehension by the Ukrainian Communists. At a conference in Taganrog in April 1918, one of the Party's ideological journals has recorded,[3] the majority of the delegates had favoured a completely independent Ukrainian Communist Party whose only link with the RKP would be the Comintern. This decision, which the journal described as a 'serious error, a concession to separatist tendencies', was to be reversed when the Ukrainian Bolsheviks met in congress in Moscow in the following July,[4] when stress was laid on the 'internationalist', as opposed to the ethnic, character of the Party's structure.

[96]

The Party organisations of all the constituent republics were subsequently incorporated in the CPSU on the same footing of complete subordination to its Central Committee. The distinction between these organisations and those of *krais* and *oblasts* is purely one of terminology: officials are directed as freely to republican Party posts as they are to posts in the *krais* and *oblasts* of the RSFSR, and some have held posts in the Party organisations of several republics. Despite the rejection of the ethnic principle, however, there is a nominal concession to nationalist sentiment in the fact that the First Secretary of the Republican Central Committee is usually (though not invariably) a native of the republic.

As has already been stated, the authority of the Party in the Soviet State was not given constitutional recognition until 1936, but the Party's monopoly of power was never in doubt before that time. A resolution of the Twelfth Party Congress in April, 1923, stated that the 'dictatorship of the working class cannot be secured otherwise than in the form of the dictatorship of its advanced vanguard, *i.e.*, the Communist Party'.[5] And although Stalin issued a disavowal a year later,[6] claiming that the expression 'dictatorship of the Party' was 'sheer nonsense' and had got into the congress resolution 'by oversight', he conceded in 1926 that 'it could be said that the dictatorship of the proletariat is *in essence* the dictatorship of its vanguard, the dictatorship of its Party in the sense that not a single important political or organisational question is decided by our Soviet and other mass organisations without guiding directions from the Party'.[7] Lenin spoke of the Communist Party as the 'ruling party',[8] and it was this term which was revived and reiterated by Khrushchev in his report to the Twentieth Party Congress in 1956.[9] The Party has consistently refused to share its power or to permit the creation of other political parties. Thus, when in 1956, after Khrushchev's denunciation of Stalin, a number of Soviet intellectuals were said to be speculating[10] on the possibility of the emergence of a second political party in the Soviet Union as the most efficacious way of preventing a new personality cult, a leading article in the official organ of the Party Central Committee stated categorically:

'With regard to our country . . . the Communist Party was, is and will be, the only ruler of thoughts, the mouthpiece of ideas and aspirations, the leader and organiser of the people throughout its struggle for Communism.'[11]

The 'guiding principle of the organisational structure of the Party' is stated to be 'democratic centralism', which is defined as follows in Article 19 of the Party Statutes (*ustav*):

(*a*) the election of all leading Party bodies from the lowest to the highest; (*b*) periodical reports of Party bodies to their Party organisations and to higher bodies; (*c*) strict Party discipline and subordination of the minority to the majority; (*d*) absolutely binding character of the decisions of higher bodies for lower bodies.

An examination of democratic centralism in practice shows that the potentially democratic character of the first three paragraphs of the definition is nullified by the centralism implicit in paragraph (*d*). The 'democratic' element should manifest itself in elections and activity reports. The characteristic method of selecting Party leaders, however, is by co-option and designation from above and not by election from below. The election of Secretaries of an *okrug* city or *raion* Party Committee, for example, must, under the Party Statutes, be confirmed by the Committee of an *oblast* or *krai* or by the Central Committee of a Republic (Article 49). One of the chief functions of the Party Central Committee Secretariat, according to Article 38 of the Statutes, is the 'selection of cadres', *i.e.*, 'those occupying command posts in the Party'.[12]

Party elections, no less than elections to Soviets, are arranged, not as an expression of free choice, but as a device for registering assent to decisions arrived at at a higher level. The single-list system is general; and, as in the case of State elections, the authorities have at intervals to calm the recurrent doubts of Party members as to whether such a procedure is really democratic. Thus one Communist, in a letter to one of the Central Committee's journals in 1956, clearly considered it ludicrous that for elections to a Party Committee only as many candidates were put forward for election as there were vacancies to be filled. 'Is it not mere formality', he asked, 'when eleven people have to be elected out of eleven?'[13] Two years later the same journal had to devote a leading article to persuading 'certain comrades' that they were mistaken in 'assuming that elections can only be democratic when the number of candidates in the voting list is in excess of those due to be elected'.[14]

A handbook for Party members in the armed forces published in 1965 found it necessary to explain.

'One cannot consider certain comrades right who think that the essence of democracy lies merely in having more candidates on the voting lists so that some can be crossed out . . . Practice shows that in the majority of Party organisations as a result of a business-like approach and serious discussion . . . the same number of candidates appears on the lists as was decided by the meeting should be elected to the Party organ in question. And it is impossible to see here any infringements of inner-Party democracy.'[15]

The 'Instructions for the Conduct of Elections of Leading Party Organs', approved by the CPSU Central Committee in March, 1962, lay down procedure for Party elections from the level of primary organisation to that of Republic Central Committee, but say nothing about procedure for elections to the CPSU Central Committee or its organs. Though Article 24 of the Party Statutes says: 'Elections to Party organs are carried out by secret ballot', the Instructions provide for secret elections only for the less important posts: members of Party committees, and delegates to Party conferences at all levels; and for open elections for the more important, executive posts: secretaries and members of bureaux of all Party committees (except the members of bureaux of primary organisations and secretaries of primary organisations where there is no bureau) and the chairmen of all Revision Commissions. Representatives of higher Party bodies may be present at all elections. Candidates need not be delegates at the respective Party conferences or congresses. Representatives of delegates to Party conferences and congresses at which elections are to be held may be summoned by the conference or congress presidium (which presides over the elections, and which may contain representatives of higher Party committees) to a meeting held in advance of the elections 'in order to make a preliminary selection of candidates for the new membership of the Party organ'. The candidates thus selected may then be proposed at the subsequent elections on behalf of this pre-election meeting. Clearly this is the procedure which ensures that Party elections produce the results desired by the leadership. The instructions do, however, contain the pious injunction that 'the preliminary proposal of candidates . . . does not limit the rights of delegates to propose and discuss candidates at the conference or congress itself'.

In secret elections, each delegate has the right to cross out the names of individual candidates on his voting paper or to add new names, no matter how many members it has previously been agreed shall be elected to the Party organ in question. Those candidates are elected who gain more than half the votes of those present at the meeting. If the number of those elected differs from the number it has previously been decided to elect, the meeting votes openly whether or not to alter its previous decision in accordance with the election results. If it decides not to alter its decision, secret voting takes place for a second time on the individual candidates.

The choice of people for elective posts in the Party can thus be seen as a mixture of 'election' from below and designation from above, which it is difficult to analyse in view of the secrecy that surrounds this type of operation. There are occasional references to elections in the Party Press, however, which suggest that they are not infrequently 'rigged' and that the participation of the rank-and-file members is no more than a formality. Thus, according to one article, city and *raion* Party Committees in Yaroslavl demanded to know from Secretaries of primary organisations, well in advance of the elections, who the new secretaries and bureau members were to be.[16] Another leading article, in 1954, criticised the practice among some city and *raion* Party Committees of confirming Secretaries of primary Party organisations before their election. This, it was stated, was 'obviously done out of a consideration that Communists will not vote against the decision of a higher Party organ'.[17]

An even more startling revelation of the attitude of rank-and-file members towards elections of Party officials appeared in an account of a *raion* Party conference published in the organ of the Central Committee in 1957.[18] One man was said to have banged his fist on the table and declared :'The mainspring in the *raikom* (its first Secretary) is worn out and needs replacing. ... True, this product (secretaries) is supplied from above and we can do nothing about it. ... The *oblast* Party Committee keeps Comrade Froltsov [who was subsequently re-elected] because he accepts the *obkom's* instructions and directives unquestionably and doesn't object.'

One can thus sympathise with the Party member quoted above who found it difficult to reconcile the Party election system with what is known as 'inner-Party democracy'. The same applies to the periodical reports submitted by the Party leaders to the lower bodies: no reports which incorporate policy decisions of the leadership can, except in violation of paragraph (d) above, be rejected or even criticised, but must be enforced.

The organisational practices of the Party are said to be based on 'inner-Party democracy'. The phrase has never been explicitly defined, but the Party Statutes make plain that it is not to be taken to imply complete freedom of discussion. Article 26 states that 'free and business-like discussion of questions of Party policy ... is the inalienable right of every Party member', but qualifies this 'right' with a paragraph which declares:

'Wide discussion, especially discussion on an All-Union scale, of questions of Party policy must be so organised ... as to preclude attempts to form fractional groupings which break the unity of the Party, attempts to split the Party.'

It follows from this that no discussion will be tolerated that could lead to an organised challenge to the Party leadership. In practice, the freedom allowed to Party members permits only the discussion of the *methods of applying* the decisions of the leading organs.

The Party Statutes state (Article 1) that 'Membership of the Communist Party of the Soviet Union is open to any citizen of the Soviet Union who accepts the Party's Programme and Statutes, actively participates in the construction of Communism, works in one of the organisations of the Party, fulfils Party decisions, and pays membership dues'. The Constitution, on the other hand, states that those who 'voluntarily unite in the Communist Party of the Soviet Union' are the 'most active and politically-conscious citizens', and the practice of recruitment likewise reveals a more restrictive policy of admittance to membership. A recruit is first admitted for a probationary period of one year as 'candidate-member', and to qualify for this he must submit recommendations from three Party members who have a Party standing of at least five years and who know him from having worked with him for not less than one year (Statutes, Articles 4 and 15). The object of the probationary period is stated to be to give applicants an opportunity to familiarise themselves with the Party Programme and Statutes and the tactics of the Party and to enable Party organisations to test the candidate's personal qualities (Article 14).

An application for admission to candidate-membership is discussed at a general meeting of a primary Party organisation and, if it is supported by two-thirds of the votes is accepted without endorsement by a higher Party organ. (Article 4 (b)).

The candidate-member takes part in the meetings of his primary organisation, though without the power to vote. After his year's probation, provided he is regarded as suitable, he may apply for full membership by going through the whole process a second time. The lower age unit for membership is 18 (Article 4), though people up to the age of 23 may only join the Party through the Komsomol (Young Communist League). The obligation of members and candidates to pay monthly dues is laid down in Article 70 of the Statutes. They are assessed on a progressive scale ranging from 10 kopeks to 3 per cent of monthly salary. In addition there is an entrance fee of two per cent of monthly salary on admission as candidate-member.

The duties demanded of a Party member are manifold and exacting. He must, *inter alia*, set an example at work; carry out Party decisions firmly and steadfastly; explain Party policy to the masses; master Marxism-Leninism; combat bourgeois ideology, private property mentality, religious beliefs, nationalism and chauvinism; strengthen the Party's unity and prevent its infiltration by people unworthy to be Communists; be vigilant and guard secrets; practise criticism and self-criticism; inform Party bodies up to the Central Committee of any actions harmful to the Party; ensure the proper selection of personnel according to political and personal qualifications; strengthen the defence potential of the USSR, and struggle for international peace and friendship (Article 2). As the Deputy Chairman of the Party Control Committee wrote in 1957: 'Our Party is a militant, centralised organisation. It disposes of all its members and decides where any particular Communist is to work. The Communist regards the decisions of the Party as a military order, goes where the Party sends him, and works to the utmost of his ability in any job.'[19]

The Party member is also stated in Article 3 of the Statutes to have certain rights: to elect and be elected to Party bodies; to discuss Party policy at Party meetings or in the Party Press, and uphold his opinion as long as the Party organisation concerned has not adopted a decision; to criticise any Party member irrespective of his position at Party meetings; to be present when his own conduct is under discussion, and to put questions, statements of views or proposals to any Party body, up to the Central Committee. In practice, however, these rights tend to be negated by the far more numerous obligations of a disciplinary character.

Communist propaganda frequently cites, as evidence of the existence of 'inner-Party democracy', the numerous instances of criticism and self-criticism which appear in the Party Press; but what it does not mention is the carefully defined limits within which criticism is permitted or encouraged. It usually takes the form of revelations of inefficiency, bureaucracy and neglect of duty or responsibility, but is directed at levels of the Party and Government hierarchy below the top ruling group. Criticism from below, despite the frequency with which the phrase is employed in Communist propaganda, is, by the very nature of the power structure in the Communist Party, an extremely rare phenomenon. In the Party, as in any other rigidly organised hierarchy of authority, criticism of a higher-ranking official or body can always be represented as a breach of discipline. The available evidence suggests that criticism in the Party is almost invariably directed downwards. A rank-and-file member or official ventures to criticise a leading official at his own level or a higher one only when he feels confident of the support of people at a still higher level of authority; so that what may appear as criticism from below is an oblique form of criticism from above. Properly regulated, therefore, criticism and self-criticism constitute an extremely useful in-strument in the hands of the Party leadership and may be said to be the Communist substitute for free discussion. They have the virtue of providing a controlled outlet for feelings of resentment and frustration among the rank and file, which may be directed with beneficial effect against targets in the lower ranks of the Party and Government hierarchy without develop-ing into organised criticism of the régime itself or bringing into question the infallibility of the Party leadership.

SOURCES

1. *KPSS v Rezolyutsiyakh*, 1953, Vol. I, p. 529.
2. *Ibid.*, p. 443.
3. *Voprosy Istorii KPSS*, No. 3, 1958, p. 44.
4. *Ibid.*, p. 47.
5. *KPSS v Rezolyutsiyakh*, 1953, Vol. I, p. 683.
6. Stalin, *Works*, Vol. 6, p. 270.
7. Stalin, *Problems of Lenin-ism*, p. 168.
8. Lenin, *Sochineniya*, 3rd edn., Vol. XXVI, p. 208.
9. *Pravda*, February 15, 1956.
10. *Il Messaggero*, May 27, 1956.

11. *Pravda*, July 6, 1956.
12. Stalin, *Problems of Leninism*, p. 784.
13. *Partiinaya Zhizn*, No. 16, 1956, p. 49.
14. *Partiinaya Zhizn*, No. 19, 1958, p. 7.
15. *Spravochnik Partiinogo Aktivista*, p. 144.

16. *Kommunist*, No. 9, 1956, p. 65.
17. *Partiinaya Zhizn*, No. 12, 1954.
18. *Pravda*, January 21, 1957.
19. *Kommunist*, No. 8, 1957 (article by I. Boitsov).

VIII

Organisation of the Party

The structural arrangement of the Party is that of a power pyramid in which the various units, except the lowest, correspond to the main territorial units of the Soviet system, and in which a Party organisation serving a given area is regarded as superior to any Party organisation which serves only part of that area (Statutes, Article 20). The broad base of the pyramid is made up of the primary Party organisations (known as 'cells' before the 1939 revision of the Statutes) which are based not on territorial units but on units of economic or occupational activity, *i.e.*, the factory, collective or State farm, units of the armed forces, offices, educational establishments, etc. Above the primary organisations rise the diminishing tiers of the Party organisations in the *raions*, towns, *okrugs*, *oblasts*, *krais* and Union Republics, culminating in the central All-Union Party organs at the apex of the pyramid.

The traditional structure of the Party apparatus was disrupted during the last two years of Khrushchev's rule by his reform of November, 1962, which split it at the middle levels into agricultural and industrial branches; and by the subsequent replacement of *raion* Party Committees by Party Committees in agricultural production directorates. The bifurcation of the apparatus 'according to the production principle' was officially justified as a method of improving Party control of the economy. It cannot have had much appeal for the many '*apparatchiki*' whose position it disturbed, and was the first of Khrushchev's reforms to be dismantled by his successors, in November, 1964.

The changes in the structure of the Soviets and the electoral system brought about by the 1936 Constitution did not lead to any parallel adjustments in the Party system. Consequently there are still three divisions of authority and responsibility in Party units at all levels, and the representative bodies are still chosen by multi-stage indirect elections.

First, the representative or so-called 'highest leading organ' for the primary organisation is the general Party meeting, held in most cases at least once a month; the Party conference or general meeting for the *okrug*, town, or *raion* organisation (once in two years); the Party conference for the *oblast* or *krai* organisation (once every two years); the Party Congress in the case of the Union Republic Parties (once in four years); and the Party Congress (once in four years) for the Communist Party of the Soviet Union (Statutes, Articles 22, 30, 44, 48, 55). At the 23rd CPSU Congress in 1966 the Statutes were amended to provide for the holding 'when necessary' of All-Union Party Conferences 'to discuss urgent questions of Party policy', and for Republican Party Conferences (Article 40). All-Union Party Conferences had been abolished in 1952. The Statutes also provide (Articles 31, 44, 48) that extraordinary conferences and congresses at the various levels may be convened either by the relevant Party committee (or Central Committee in the case of Republican Parties and the CPSU) or at the request of one-third of the members of the relevant Party organisation (or, in the case of the All-Union Congress, one-third of the total number of members represented at the previous congress). The general meetings of primary organisations choose the delegates to the town or *raion* conferences, which elect delegates to the *okrug*, *oblast* and *krai* conferences and the congresses of the Union-Republican Parties, which in turn elect delegates to the All-Union Party Congress. Further statutory functions of the conferences and congresses at territorial levels and at the centre are the approval of the reports of their Party committees (Central Committees) and revision (auditing) commissions and the election of new ones (Articles 32, 44, 48).

    Second, from the town and *raion* upwards, there is an 'executive organ' charged with directing 'all the current work of the organisation' and elected by the above representative bodies from among their number (Article 23): in town, *raion*, *okrug*, *oblast* and *krai* organisations this is known as the Party Committee; in Union Republic organisations and at the All-Union level it is called a Central Committee. Town, *raion* and *okrug* committees are required to meet in plenary session at least once in three months (Article 47, 51), *oblast* and *krai* committees and Central Committees of Union Republic Parties once in four months (Article 46), and the Central Committee of the CPSU once in six months (Article 37). The general meeting of a primary organisation of not less than 15 members annually elects a bureau to deal with current business; otherwise it elects only a secretary and deputy secretary (Article 56).

Third, there are the smaller, inner bodies, the bureaux and their secretaries, which Party Committees and Central Committees elect and which, since they are in permanent or frequent session and constantly engaged in Party business at all territorial levels and at the centre, exercise the greatest influence on the day-to-day operation of the whole Party apparatus.

THE CENTRAL ORGANS OF THE PARTY

The 'supreme organ' of the CPSU is stated by the Party Statutes to be the Party Congress (Article 30). During the 13 years from 1939 to 1952 it never met, although supposed to do so every three years. In 1952 the Statutes were amended to provide that regular congresses should be convened not less than once in four years, and extraordinary congresses convened by the Central Committee itself or at the request of one-third of the members represented at the last congress (Article 30). The functions of the Congress are: to 'hear and confirm' the reports of the Central Committee, Central Revision (Auditing) Commission and 'other central organisations'; to 'review, amend and endorse' the Party programme and Statutes; to 'determine the line of the Party in matters of home and foreign policy and examine and decide the most important questions of Communist construction', and to elect the Central Committee and Central Revision Commission (Article 32).

Under the Party Statutes 'norms of representation' at congresses are laid down by the Central Committee (Article 30). For the 23rd Congress it ordered that there should be a delegate with a 'decisive' vote for every 2,500 Party members and one with a 'consultative' vote for every 2,500 candidate-members.[1] On this basis 4,820 voting delegates and 323 with a 'consultative' vote, representing 11,673,676 Party members and 797,403 candidates, were elected to the 23rd Congress.[2]

Since Stalin established his dictatorship the Party Congress has had no independent significance. In practice, it is used almost entirely by the leadership group for the announcement of important new developments in the Party line, while the presence of delegations from 'fraternal' parties abroad is highlighted as a symbol of the 'international solidarity' of the Communist movement, of which the Soviet Union is the fountain-head. There is no effective discussion; speeches bear all the signs of having been concerted in advance, and all decisions are taken 'unanimously' to preserve the myth of 'monolithic unity'.

Although in theory it was the Central Committee which was supposed to be subjecting itself to the scrutiny and examination of the Party, the 23rd Congress of 1966 took the form of a monologue by the Central Committee, which in effect controlled and predetermined the entire proceedings. Of the 68 Soviet speakers who addressed the congress only 16 were not members of the outgoing Central Committee and Revision Commission, and only five were not elected to the new Central Committee and Revision Commission.

The 'directing organs' of the Congress (Presidium, Secretariat, Editorial Commission and Mandate Commission) consisted almost entirely of members and candidate-members of the Central Committee, nominated by other members of the Central Committee. The 'Council of representatives of delegations of Party organisations of *oblasts, krais* and republics', in whose name the appointments to the 'directing organs' were made, doubtless consisted of the heads of those delegations, who, with few exceptions, were either members or candidate-members of the Central Committee.[3]

The agenda of the congress, although it is formally confirmed at the opening session, is also determined by the Central Committee and announced several months in advance. For the 23rd Congress it was as follows.

1. Report of the Central Committee, delivered by Brezhnev;
2. Report of the Central Revision Commission, delivered by its chairman, N. A. Muraveva;
3. Directives for the Five-Year National Economic Plan (1966–70), presented by Kosygin;
4. Election of Central Party organs.

Endorsement of the Five-Year Plan is largely a formality, which merely emphasises the rubber-stamp nature of the congress. The directives had already been approved by the Central Committee at its February, 1966, Plenum before being presented to the 23rd Congress. The procedures for the election of the Central Party organs are not made public. It is most likely at the nomination stage that the wishes of the ruling group are made known and the elections virtually decided. It is difficult otherwise to explain how the occupants of certain key Party posts throughout the Soviet Union, hand-picked by the First Secretary, are so consistently successful in elections to the central organs.

The business of a congress is not necessarily confined to the published agenda. Khrushchev's denunciation of Stalin, for example, occurred in a report delivered to a 'closed' session of the 20th Congress on 25th February 1956, although the Soviet Press made no reference to it. The official stenographic account records the fact, though not the substance, of the report and also the resolution adopted thereon.[4]

Of the two bodies elected by the Party Congress—the Central Committee and the Central Revision Commission—the latter is of minor importance. According to the Statutes (Article 36) it supervises the expeditious and proper handling of affairs by the central bodies of the Party and audits the accounts of the Treasury and the enterprises of the Central Committee of the CPSU. Its Chairman reports to the congress for the period under review on the efficiency of the Party apparatus and on such matters as the collection of membership dues and revenues from the Party Press, etc., and the allocation of funds for various purposes (quoting only percentage figures); the efficiency of the Party periphery in carrying out its various tasks of propaganda, Party education, etc.; the processing of letters and complaints addressed to Party organisations; cases of loss of Party documents, etc.

The Central Committee is, in theory at least, a far more important institution. It consists of full and candidate-members. The latter have only a 'consultative' voice, *i.e.* they attend sessions of the Central Committee and take part in its deliberations but do not have a vote (Statutes, Article 37). Once the Central Committee has been elected it becomes a closed body in the sense that no provision is made in the Statutes for the co-option of new members between congresses. They lay down that in the event of the 'departure' (*vybytie*) of a member from the Central Committee his place shall be filled 'from among' the candidate-members (Article 33), 'Departure' may take the form of death, expulsion from the Party or from its Central Committee. Expulsions from membership or candidate membership of the Central Committee are decided between congresses at a plenum of the Central Committee by a two-thirds majority of the full members (Article 25).

The composition of the central organs is, in practice, largely determined by status. In the case of the Central Committee the holders of certain public offices, such as the First Secretaryship of republic, *krai* and certain key *oblast* and city Party Committees and the more important Government organs seem automatically to qualify for membership, and no doubt suitability for Central Committee membership is one of the major factors determining who shall occupy certain posts. Conversely, since their 'election' to the Central Committee is *ex officio*, their removal from that body almost certainly follows at the next plenum should they lose their posts. The power to influence an appointment carrying Central Committee status is therefore an important political asset for an individual leader. Of the 195 full members of the Central Committee 'elected' at the 23rd Congress 20 were in the Central Party apparatus, 70 were Secretaries of republic, *krai, oblast* or major city Committees (including the First Secretaries of all the republics and *krais*), and 40 occupied Deputy Ministerial, Ministerial or higher posts in the Central Government.

The Statutes state that 'Between congresses the Central Committee of the CPSU directs all the activities of the Party and the local Party organs; selects and appoints leading functionaries; directs the work of central government bodies and public organisations of working people through the Party groups in them; sets up various Party organs, institutions and enterprises and directs their activities; appoints editorial boards of the central newspapers and journals functioning under its control; and distributes the funds of the Party budget and controls its execution.' It also 'represents the CPSU in its relations with other parties' (Article 34). Its theoretical powers are thus virtually all-embracing and between congresses it is the supreme Party authority.

But after its first post-revolutionary election in March, 1918,[5] it followed a course of increasing size, less frequent meetings and declining powers. A resolution of the Party's 8th Congress in March, 1919, fixed its membership at 19, including eight candidates, and stipulated that it meet in plenary session not less than twice a month.[6] Unlike other executive bodies (*e.g.* the Presidium) the Central Committee has expanded consistently without any reversal of the process. The 23rd Congress in 1966 elected a Central Committee of 195 and 165 full members and candidates respectively. From 1921, plenums were required to be held once in two months,[7] from 1934 once in four months,[8] and from 1952 once in six months. At present this last requirement seems to be observed, although a plenum held in December, 1956, was four months late, owing, as subsequent events showed, to an unsettled dispute in the Presidium. Even so the post-1953 record is an improvement on the Stalinist era. Khrushchev is reported to have told the 20th Congress that during the last 15 years of Stalin's life plenums were hardly ever called and that not a single plenum took place during the war.[9] Apart from the one plenum said to have taken place in January, 1944, to adopt a new National Anthem and to allow Union Republics to maintain armed forces and establish direct foreign relations, the published record seems to confirm his statement.[10] It is certainly the case, to judge by the official record, that the plenum of February, 1947, was the only one held between the end of the war and Stalin's death.[11]

Since 1953 Central Committee plenums appear to have been used primarily, like congresses, for announcements of changes of policy by the Party leaders and also for progress reports. The main decisions of importance, both economic and political, have been taken during these meetings, which have usually shortly preceded, and determined the agenda of, meetings of the Supreme Soviet.

The most important recent Plenum was that on October 14, 1964, reported by *Pravda* two days later, which 'released' Khrushchev from his offices of First Secretary of the CPSU Central Committee and member of its Presidium and Chairman of the USSR Council of Ministers 'in connexion with his advanced age and the deterioration of his health'. No details of how the Plenum arrived at this momentous decision have been published. We have only Brezhnev's word for it that 'It was held amidst the complete unanimity of all its participants.'[12] This may have been true if, as seems likely, the Plenum was held merely to sanction a *coup* prepared in the utmost secrecy by Khrushchev's opponents in the Presidium. Brezhnev went on to claim, without any supporting evidence, that 'the decisions of the Plenum met the approval and support of the entire Party and the entire Soviet people.'[13]

A certain number of documents are published over the signature of the Central Committee without a plenum being announced: *e.g.* draft directives of the 20th Congress on the Sixth Five-Year Plan,[14] announcement of the dissolution of the Cominform,[15] decree on the elimination of the personality cult and its consequences[16] and the decree on preparations for celebration of the centenary of the First International.[17] Such decisions are probably taken by the Presidium or the Secretariat, perhaps after consultation with members of the Central Committee. The Central Committee decision of March 9, 1957, changing the editorial board of the journal *Voprosy Istorii*,[18] for example, was said to have been reached *after long discussion in the Secretariat.*[19]

The way in which decisions are reached at plenums is shrouded in mystery. The edited accounts of certain plenums published since December, 1958, throw little light on how differences are resolved. Whether there is genuine debate in the Central Committee on the reports submitted by the Presidium or the Secretariat or whether the Presidium has sufficient authority to bulldoze its plans through the Central Committee it is not possible to know with certainty, though it must be stated that the Presidium has never been overthrown by the Central Committee. On the other hand, though the size of the Central Committee makes it too clumsy to be an effectively operative body, it certainly now acts as a sounding-board and, as the June Plenum of 1957 showed, may also develop into a court of reference. When the Central Committee expelled Beriya in 1953 and Zhukov in October, 1957, it did so with the agreement, and clearly on the initiative, of the other members of the Presidium. But when in June, 1957, a real conflict developed between two groups in the Presidium the Central Committee was called in to arbitrate—and in so doing may have created a precedent capable of enhancing its future importance.

According to the Statutes (Article 38), the Central Committee elects a Politburo to direct the 'work of the Party between Central Committee plenums', a Secretariat to direct 'current work, chiefly in the selection of cadres and the verification of execution of decisions'; and a Secretary-General. The results of the elections to these highest Party offices, but no indication of how they were achieved, are announced after the Central Committee's First Plenum following the Party Congress.

For the greater part of its history the Central Committee has had, in addition to its Secretariat, two bureaux—the policy and organisation bureaux (Politburo and Orgburo) originally of five members each, set up at the 8th Congress in March, 1919.[20] The Politburo was to decide matters which did not admit of delay, and report to the fortnightly plenums of the Central Committee. The Orgburo was to report similarly on 'organisational work'.[21] As Lenin pointed out at the 9th Congress in March, 1920, most questions could be represented as policy matters, and the practice had developed whereby at the request of one member of the Central Committee any matter could come within the purview of the Politburo.[22] The latter, for obvious reasons, soon outstripped the Orgburo (abolished in 1952) in importance and became the most powerful political body in the country. But, as Stalin established his personal dictatorship, even this select body, if we are to believe Khrushchev, ceased to be consulted about his personal decisions on matters of substance or even informed about them.[23] On the same evidence we learn that Stalin destroyed the collective nature of the Politburo by forming among its members small groups to deal with separate aspects of the work, with the result that certain members were excluded from participation in the reaching of decisions. One member, A. A. Andreyev, was said to have been debarred by Stalin altogether from participating in the Politburo's work, and another, Voroshilov, could only attend meetings with Stalin's permission.[24]

At the 19th Congress in 1952 the Politburo was replaced by a new body, the Presidium of the Central Committee, with a greatly enlarged membership: 25 members and 11 candidates instead of 11 members and one candidate. The proposal for the increase was Stalin's,[25] and most of the new members were of the younger generation whom he himself had trained. Among the full and candidate-members of the Presidium were all 10 of the Central Committee Secretaries and all 13 of the Deputy Chairmen of the USSR Council of Ministers, *i.e.*, the commanding heights of Party and State administration were apparently merged in the manner advocated by Lenin.[26] But a more plausible explanation of this infusion of new blood into the Presidium membership was Stalin's desire to dilute its power and minimise the risk of concerted opposition from the old Politburo members. That the power of this expanded Presidium was more apparent than real became clear immediately after Stalin's death, when it was revealed that there had also existed another inner body—the Bureau of the Presidium—for which there was no provision in the Party Statutes but which must have been the real nucleus of power.[27]

After Stalin's death the Bureau of the Presidium was abolished and the Presidium itself reduced to 10 members, among whom only Malenkov and Khrushchev were also members of the Secretariat. But the former soon gave up his secretarial post to devote himself entirely to the Premiership. All the other members of the Presidium occupied State posts. The decisions of March, 1953, thus gave incontestable pre-eminence to the Presidium (preponderantly composed of State officials) and a secondary rôle to the Secretariat (the centre of Party administration).

But after abandoning, voluntarily or under pressure, the key position in the Secretariat Malenkov progressively declined in influence; while Khrushchev, making full use of his powers of appointment, gradually consolidated his control over the Party apparatus. From the time he was named First Secretary at the September, 1953, plenum of the Central Committee, at which he presented the report on agriculture, he began to emerge as the spokesman of the Presidium and the Central Committee. He presented a further agricultural report to the plenum of January, 1955, and a few days later Malenkov resigned from the Premiership, pleading errors he had allegedly committed in the direction of agriculture.

The fact that after the 20th Congress in 1956 the Presidium of 11 members was re-elected in its entirety, despite the obvious differences between them (both Malenkov and Molotov were obliquely criticised at the congress), throws some light on the methods that must be used for choosing the Presidium/Politburo. The Party Statutes state that all Party organs must be elected by secret ballot and that each candidate must be voted on separately. If this injunction were literally carried out and the members of the Central Committee really had a free vote, there would be no control over what team they would choose. In practice, therefore, the Presidium/Politburo must give them guidance. This virtually pre-supposes a unanimous recommendation on the part of the Presidium/Politburo members, accompanied, it may well be imagined, by a process of bargaining. So long as no one person or group in the Presidium/Politburo was absolutely supreme this would naturally lead to the proposal for re-election of all the existing members. Thus, while the balance of power exists, the Presidium/Politburo tends to become a self-perpetuating organ.

When in June, 1957, the 'anti-Party group' challenged Khrushchev's policies in the Presidium, a struggle ensued in which Khrushchev was able to appeal to the supporters with whom, using his powers of appointment, he had packed the Central Committee. The 15 members of the new Presidium elected after the expulsion of the 'anti-Party group' contained no fewer than ten members of the Central Committee Secretariat, an imbalance in favour of the Party apparatus which became even more pronounced when Khrushchev replaced Bulganin as Chairman of the Council of Ministers in March, 1958.

The proceedings of the Party Presidium/Politburo are never published and there is little available information on how its decisions are arrived at. The only public reference to this question occurred in Khrushchev's interview in May, 1957, with the Managing Editor of the *New York Times*.[28] According to Khrushchev, the Presidium met at least once a week, and serious discussion took place. The members 'usually arrive at a common viewpoint', but if they do not 'decisions are taken by a simple majority vote'. As a result of a revision of the Party Statutes at the 23rd Congress in 1966 the Presidium reverted to its old name, Politburo. So far no evidence has appeared that this change of nomenclature had any deeper significance.

When the Secretariat was instituted at the 8th Congress in 1919 its powers were not defined,[29] but they evolved rapidly in practice. At the 9th Congress a year later the Secretariat was strengthened by the introduction of three permanent secretaries from among the members of the Central Committee, and its authority was enhanced by the transfer to it from the Orgburo of responsibility for 'current questions of an organisational and executive character',[30] including the staffing of the Party and State systems with reliable personnel. It was at this point that the Secretariat began to develop into something more than a mere executive organ putting into effect the decisions of the Central Committee. Stalin's appointment as Secretary-General in 1922 meant that a strong personality became associated with a focally placed office, which, as the co-ordinating link between the Politburo and the Orgburo, became in effect the strategic hub of the Party. When the top structure of the Party was reorganised at the 19th Congress in 1952, the Orgburo was abolished and its functions were taken over by the Secretariat. But the adjustment of the Statutes this necessitated, Khrushchev implied at the time, represented only the formal acceptance of what had already taken place in fact.[31] The scope of the Secretariat's work was also further enlarged by its absorption of one of the functions assigned to the Party Control Commission by the 1939 Statutes, namely that of checking the fulfilment of Party decisions.

The 23rd Congress in 1966 restored the post of Secretary-General, which Stalin, who had held it for 30 years, quietly dropped at the 19th Congress in 1952; and abolished the title, First Secretary, first assumed by Khrushchev in September, 1953. This change, like the substitution of Politburo for Presidium, has been officially represented as a return to Leninist ways, though the readopted nomenclature is far more closely associated with Stalin.

The vast 'apparatus' or official full-time staff of the Party is ascribed to the Central Committee, but in practice it has been directed by the Secretariat, itself nominally an organ of the Central Committee, under Stalin as Secretary-General, under Khrushchev as First Secretary and now under Brezhnev as Secretary-General. The strength and determinative influence of the Secretariat have derived precisely from the fact that it is permanently and exclusively preoccupied with Party affairs. For obvious reasons the official engaged exclusively on Party business enjoys a distinct advantage over the rank-and-file member employed in a factory or a Government office. The Party apparatus therefore soon developed into the centre of initiative, direction and control. This was the case at all levels of the Party hierarchy. Both at the centre and in the lower Party organisations authority was, in practice, transferred from the representative organs (the congresses or conferences) to the committees or Central Committee they had formally elected and thence to the Party Secretaries, who ostensibly were responsible to them and executed their will. The key rôle of the central Secretariat has developed out of its personnel responsibilities and its authority to supervise the activity of local Party organisations. Since secretarial appointments and promotions in Party organisations are within the gift of the central apparatus a secretarial hierarchy has emerged with a vested interest in showing allegiance to the First Party Secretary/Secretary-General. He, in turn, by employing his powers of patronage to promote his most reliable supporters to key posts in the provinces which carry Central Committee membership, can enhance his chances of dominating the Party Congress, securing endorsement of his policies, and eliminating real or potential opposition from the centre of power. As the careers of both Stalin and Khrushchev have confirmed, control of the Central Committee Secretariat can be an invaluable asset for anyone aiming at supreme power.

The Central Committee is required by the Statutes to form a third organ, the Party Control Committee (Article 39). Its duties are defined in the Statutes as maintaining a check on the observance of Party discipline by members and candidate-members, bringing to account those guilty of violating the Party Programme and Statutes, Party and State discipline or Party morality, and the hearing of appeals against reprimands and expulsions from the Party ordered by *obkoms* and *kraikoms* and Central Committees of Union Republics. The committee's duties are thus primarily concerned with supervising the personal activities of Party members. At various periods in its history the committee (sometimes designated a Commission) has however been assigned wider functions and powers. Thus, before 1952 it was charged with supervising the fulfilment by Party organisations and Soviet and economic organs of decisions of the Party and Central Committee and with checking the work of local Party organisations.[32] These powers passed to the Secretariat in 1952; but the Control Committee's authority as a Party watchdog was increased by the new right to have its own representatives independent of the local Party organs, in republics, *krais* and *oblasts*.[33] This last provision was deleted from the Statutes at the 20th Congress of 1956,[34] and the Committee's importance was further reduced in November, 1962, when Khrushchev set up a new Party-State Control Committee under Shelepin with an extensive network of controllers empowered to investigate both government and Party organs. The abolition of Shelepin's committee in December, 1965, seems to have restored to the Control Committee some of its former importance, though it still appears to be confined to dealing with the personal behaviour of Party members.

[117]

The Party Statutes adopted in 1934 and 1939 specified the departmental organisations of the Party staff which should exist at the centre and at the various subordinate levels.[35] Since 1952, however, these provisions have been dropped from the Statutes, and the only clues to the present structure of the apparatus and the functions of the departments occur in isolated Press references to officials working inside it and in an account published by an Italian Communist Party delegation of its interviews with certain Soviet Communist Party officials.[36] It appears that the Central Party apparatus includes departments for Organisational Party Work; Propaganda; Information; Culture; Science and Educational Establishments; Agriculture; Transport and Communications; Heavy Industry; Machine-building; Light and Food Industry; Defence Industry; Chemical Industry; Construction; Administrative Organs; Trade and Everyday Services; Financial and Planning Organs; International; Liaison with the Communist and Workers' Parties of Socialist Countries; Foreign Cadres; and General. For a number of years under Khrushchev several of these departments were duplicated, separate ones having been established for the RSFSR on the one hand and for the remaining Union Republics on the other.

The Departments for the RSFSR came under the control of the Bureau of the Central Committee of the CPSU for the RSFSR, set up in 1956 and presided over by Khrushchev, and abolished at the 23rd Congress in 1966. A further complication under Khrushchev was that the bifurcation of the Party into agricultural and industrial branches also affected the Central Committee apparatus. Separate bureaux were set up for agriculture and industry and some Central Committee departments were also bifurcated (there appeared, for example, a 'Department for agricultural Party organs in the RSFSR'), and there also emerged an RSFSR Bureau for Industry and an RSFSR Bureau for Agriculture.

Within the central Party apparatus the organisational Party work department occupies a pivotal position, being concerned with the placement of the more important cadres. It pronounces on the suitability or otherwise of officials nominated for work in other departments of the Central Party apparatus and of candidates for State appointments, ranging from Ministerial posts in the Governments of the Union Republics down to the level of Chairman and Deputy Chairman of *oblast* Soviets (lower-ranking posts come under the jurisdiction of the local Party organs), and supervises the allocation of Party cadres in the trade unions and in public organisations generally. It maintains a card index of all Party leaders and functionaries, and submits recommendations to the Central Committee concerning modification of the composition of the Party organisations. This control from the centre is said to be necessary, among other things, because of the tendency of local organisations to overstaff themselves. The department also supervises and controls their activities from the point of view of ensuring the correct application of the Party political line and the observance of the Party Statutes, etc.[37] Another of its main functions is close control over the rate and quality of Party recruitment. Its office for Party enrolment distributes membership cards—identical for all parts of the Soviet Union—to the various organisations and controls their issue to Party members. While it is the primary organisation the *raikom* or *gorkom* which decides the admission of new Party members, the organisational Party work department can recommend the acceptance (or, by inference, the rejection) of an application for membership. The office for Party enrolment controls recruitment in the RSFSR and other Union Republics, and maintains a complete list of members of the CPSU in numerical order.[38]

Finally, the department controls the work of the central, inter-*oblast* and Republic Party schools, training personnel for Party, trade union and Soviet work, and selects the students for them.[39]

Among the other departments whose designations give little indication of their total area of responsibility and whose functions can only be inferred from references in the Press, is the Administrative Organs Department. It appears to deal, *inter alia*, with the organs of the Procurator's Office, the courts, State Control, internal affairs and State security. The functions of the department for Foreign Cadres seem to include the selection, vetting and control of Soviet citizens who are posted abroad to work on construction projects or as experts or advisers in foreign aid schemes.

Most of the departments of the CPSU Central Committee concerned with internal affairs have lower-level replicas in the Republican Central Committees, and the more important ones are represented territorially throughout the Party structure down to *gorkom* and *raikom* level. For example, the Leningrad *gorkom* in 1966 had at least eight departments: organisational Party work; propaganda and agitation; administrative, trade and finance organs; industry and transport; schools; construction and urban economy; science and culture; and light industry and food.

The main purpose of the Central Committee departments is stated to be to give aid and advice to the peripheral organisations in carrying out their duties, and for this purpose use is made of circulars, letters, the Party Press and regular visits by instructors, who are said to spend three-quarters of their time away from their departments.[40] The Italian Communist Party was told in 1958 that there had been some devolution of power from the centre to the local organisations. Whereas formerly nominations of heads of departments of Republican Central Committees, of directors of large concerns, scientific and university institutes and of Chairmen of Soviet Executive Committees in the Republics had required the confirmation of the Central Committee of the CPSU, the Republican Central Committees were said to be autonomous in this matter.[41]

The Party budget is centralised and is approved by the Central Committee of the CPSU, as are the budgets of the Union Republic Central Committees. The proportion of paid officials remains a secret, and questions on this subject by the Italian Communist delegation were evasively met with the claim that since the war their number had been greatly reduced. In primary organisations with less than 100 members work was entirely voluntary; in those with over 100 members the Secretary at least is paid. For primary organisations with over 1,000 members there was no special ruling, the number of paid officials depending on the scale and pressure of work, but they usually included a Secretary and one or two Deputy Secretaries. In the Party factory committee at the Kuibyshev power station, which controlled 3,500 Communists, there were a Secretary, two Deputy Secretaries, a group of inspectors, a propagandist and a lecturer.[42]

There were said to be 29,000 salaried Party functionaries in primary organisations before a reduction of the apparatus announced in June, 1957, and this number was to have been decreased by about 6,000.[43] On the other hand, the Party Press has revealed the enormous increase during recent years in the number of 'exempted' *i.e.* paid secretaries of primary organisations. Between 1940 and 1957 their number increased five times, while that of primary organisations as a whole had only doubled; and in some Party organisations (*e.g.* that of Tadzhikistan) their number increased not less than 15-fold.[44] It was claimed that Khrushchev's reorganisation of the Party in November, 1962, brought a reduction of 10 per cent. in the number of permanent Party officials, and that paid officials remained in only seven per cent. of primary Party organisations.[45] What happened when the reorganisation was scrapped in November, 1964, has not been divulged.

The secrecy surrounding the size of the full-time Party staff makes it impossible to gauge with accuracy the wastefulness of the duplication of the State administration. All the indications are, however, that the amount of expert talent engaged in purely Party functions is considerable and must constitute, if one considers the economic aspect alone, an extravagant drain on the country's manpower resources which only a totalitarian régime could countenance. The information published by the Italian Communist delegation contains a number of statistics which give some idea of the size of the staffs of local Party organisations. Thus in the Smolny *raion* of Leningrad (which is only one of 16 *raions* in that city) there were no fewer than 85 paid Party functionaries, including four *raikom* Secretaries, 40 Secretaries of primary organisations and 41 officials in the *raikom* departmental apparatus.[46] In the rural *raion* of Brovary, near Kiev, there were 28 Party functionaries made up of four *raikom* Secretaries and 24 departmental functionaries (the number of paid primary organisation Secretaries was not given).[47] The size of the apparatus of the Stalingrad *gorkom* was not given, but of the *gorkom* members alone 25 were Party functionaries (including six *raikom* Secretaries).[48] Finally, while the size of the Stalino *obkom* apparatus was not given (and it must have been substantial) one-third of the 150 members and candidate-members of the *obkom* and revision commission were said to be Party *apparatchiki*.[49]

An 'exempted' Secretary of a primary organisation receives his salary, in accordance with a set scale, from the *raikom*. It was stated in 1958 that in an industrial concern he received either his previous salary as a production worker or 1,400 roubles a month, whichever was the higher.[50] A Central Committee decree of May, 1957, in the interests of economy and to stimulate voluntary work, permitted *obkoms*, *kraikoms* and Republican Central Committees to sanction the appointment, in primary organisations qualifying for an 'exempted' Secretary, of 'non-exempted'

Secretaries, who would receive as an inducement, in addition to their production pay, a supplement of from one-quarter to a half of a Secretary's salary, though not in excess of 700 roubles a month.[51] A further decree, of September, 1958, authorised local Party Committees to appoint non-staff instructors.

It is a cardinal rule that 'exempted' Secretaries of primary organisations are forbidden under any pretext to receive payment or bonuses from economic organs. As one Party journal has stated: 'The slightest violation of the independence ... of the Secretary of a primary Party organisation leads to his becoming incapable of fulfilling his duties as a political leader and of boldly developing criticism and self-criticism.'[52] Nevertheless, the instances reported in the Party Press of salaried functionaries accepting bribes in the form either of monetary awards or of appointment to fictitious but salaried posts in Ministries and factories are numerous enough to suggest that the practice has been widespread.[53]

THE LOWER PARTY ORGANS

The central organs are the repository of supreme power in the Party hierarchy, and their orders and directives control and determine the activities of all local Party organisations. Below the All-Union level, in all Republics except the RSFSR, there are the Republican Party organisations. The Congress of each Union Republic Communist Party elects a Central Committee (usually of 100–125) which in turn elects a Central Committee bureau, which includes a number of Secretaries, who must have a Party standing of not less than five years (Statutes, Article 45). The resolution on amendments to the Party Statutes, adopted by the 20th Congress of the CPSU, recognising that conditions of work vary, stated that the number of secretaries in Party Committees should not be specified in the Statutes but should be determined by the CPSU Central Committee.[54] The bureau is a body of considerable influence, being ordinarily composed of the most important personalities in the Republic, such as the Republic Party Secretaries, the Chairman of the Council of Ministers, the Chairman of the Presidium of the Supreme Soviet, the Commander of the local Military District and the First Secretaries of the more important *oblast* Party organisations. Real initiative, however, tends to be concentrated in the Secretariat, which is charged with the 'examination of current questions and the checking of fulfilment' (Article 45) and, more particularly, in the hands of the First Secretary, who is invariably appointed by the Central apparatus.

Below the Republican level, the *oblast* and *krai* Party Committees elect bureaux containing an unspecified number of Secretaries, and consisting of the most powerful people in the *oblast* or *krai*. The 13 members of the bureau of the Leningrad *obkom* in 1966 included the five *oblast* Party Secretaries, the First Secretary of the Leningrad *gorkom*, the head of the obkom Organisational Party Work Department, the Chairman of the Executive Committee of the *oblast* Soviet (*Oblispolkom*), and one of his Deputies, the Chairman of the *oblast* Trade Union Council, the Chairman of the Executive Committee of the town Soviet (*Gorispolkom*), the Commander of the Leningrad Military District; and the Head of the Leningrad KGB. The candidate-members of the Bureau were the director of the Party newspaper and the First Secretary of the *oblast* Komsomol Committee. In theory the bureau is elected in secret ballot by the *obkom*; but if the 97 full members of the Leningrad *obkom*, all presumably with strong personal aspirations to bureau membership, were really given a free vote it is unlikely that such a neat pattern of representation would be achieved. In practice, however, 'democratic centralism' as applied to the selection of key personnel seems to be the art of combining choice from above with formal ratification from below in such a way as to make this operation appear like an election.

The First Secretary of the Republic, *krai* or *oblast* Committee is a most important figure in the Party administration. He is held ultimately responsible for the efficient functioning of all the city and *raion* Party and Komsomol organisations and the State institutions, and for the plan fulfilment of all the economic enterprises which come under his jurisdiction. His continuance in office thus depends on his success in achieving efficient execution of the directives of the top Party leadership; and while it has clearly been the policy of that leadership, by means of its system of controls, to emphasise the insecurity and dependence of such local Party leaders so as to render them compliant to the orders of the central authorities, the complexity of government, in particular the need to adapt general directives to local conditions, in a country as vast as the Soviet Union necessarily invests the First Secretary with wide powers and a considerable measure of executive initiative.

[123]

The multifarious responsibilities of the lower Party organs (*i.e.* in effect, of their secretarial apparatus) are set forth in skeletal form in Article 42 of the Party Statutes. They are:

'(a) political and organisational work among the masses, mobilisation of the masses for the fulfilment of the tasks of Communist construction, for the maximum development of industrial and agricultural production, for the fulfilment and over-fulfilment of State plans; solicitude for the steady improvement of the material and cultural standards of the working people;

(b) organisation of ideological work, propaganda of Marxism-Leninism . . . guidance of the local Press, radio and television, and control over the activities of cultural and educational institutions;

(c) guidance of Soviets, trade unions, the Komsomol, the co-operatives and other public organisations . . .

(d) selection and appointment of leading personnel, their education in the spirit of communist ideas . . .

(e) large-scale enlistment of communists in the conduct of Party activities as non-staff workers, as a form of social work;

(f) organisation of various institutions and enterprises of the Party . . . distribution of Party funds within the given organisation; systematic information of the higher Party body and accountability to it for their work.'

Below *oblast* level there are the town and *raion* Party organisations, whose work is conducted between conferences by the town and *raion* Party Committees (*gorkom* and *raikom*) whose plenum is the highest Party authority between conferences. Their size is not stipulated in the Party Statutes, but it was stated in 1955 that *raikoms* usually consist of 40–50 and *gorkoms* of 50–70 members. Their total membership throughout the Soviet Union was given as exceeding 200,000.[55] These figures are no doubt rough averages and there are exceptions among the more important cities: the Moscow *gorkom*, for instance, now has 129 members and 49 candidate-members.[56] The *gorkom* (*raikom*) is required by the Statutes to elect a bureau, including the Party Committee Secretaries. These latter must have a Party standing of at least three years and their election must be confirmed by the Party Committee at the next higher instance (*oblast*, *krai* or Republic) (Article 49).

As at Republic and *oblast* levels, the bureau of the *raikom* (*gorkom*) represents a cross-section of the more influential personalities in the area. Thus the bureau of the Smolny *raikom* in Leningrad was said to consist in 1957 of the four *raikom* Secretaries, the Secretaries of two of the *raion*'s primary organisations, the Chairman of the Executive Committee of the *raion* Soviet (*raiispolkom*), the director of a scientific institute and the director of a building enterprise.[57] The nine members of the bureau of the rural *raikom* of Brovary near Kiev included the four *raikom* Secretaries, the Chairman of the *raiispolkom*, the Chairman of a collective farm and the director of the *raion* newspaper.[58] The bureau of the Stalingrad *gorkom*, also of nine members, consisted of three *gorkom* Secretaries, the Secretary of a *raikom*, the Secretary of the tractor factory Party Committee, the Secretary of the city Komsomol Committee, the head of the Industry and Transport Department of the *gorkom*, the Chairman of the Executive Committee of the city Soviet (*gorispolkom*) and the director of the city's largest factory.[59]

Theoretically the *gorkom* (*raikom*) is one of the 'organs of collective leadership in the localities' and its bureau is merely its executive organ, charged with the current implementation of business.[60] It is a characteristic of Party, as of State, practice at all levels in the Soviet Union, however, that the smaller the executive body the greater its authority in practice; and there is abundant evidence in the Soviet Press that it is not usually the bureau and the Secretariat which are controlled by the Party Committee but the reverse. A member of a Moscow *raikom* complained in a Party journal, for example, that workers in the apparatus 'regard members of the *raikom* as their assistants whom any official can summon and send off to carry out some task or other. It is wrong when the apparatus begins to order *raikom* members about, but the bureau of the *raikom* and the Secretaries frequently encourage this.'[61] The secretary of a primary organisation complained in 1958 that the bureau of a certain *gorkom* had exceeded its powers in announcing the convocation of a city Party conference before the matter had even been discussed by the plenum of the *gorkom*—the only body competent to decide on it.[62] Another Secretary of a primary organisation pointed out that the work of the *gorkom* of which he was a member was concentrated almost entirely in the hands of the bureau and the apparatus. 'The significance of the *gorkom* as a collctive organ', he emphasised, 'is reduced when its members can consider only the few questions submitted for discussion by the plenum.' The rank-and file *gorkom* members, as distinct from the more exalted bureau members, were not given Party assignments because the *apparatchiki* 'consider—they do not, of course, say so aloud—that such comrades have insufficient experience of Party-organisational work.'[63] The abuse of

[125]

delegated power is on occasions carried a stage further. Secretaries have sometimes aspired even to dictatorial powers. The First Secretary of one *raikom* was said to have tried on occasions to by-pass the bureau and to make decisions on his own: 'Matters reached the stage where the bureau considered only such matters as were put forward by Comrade Husainov, while the suggestions of the other members of the bureau were not taken into account.'[64]

The activities of the city and *raion* Party organisations reflect the work of the *oblast* and Republican organisations on a smaller scale. An important aspect of their work is the selection and approval of personnel for local Party assignments and for the more important positions in local government, the Komsomol and trade unions, etc. Their influence is ordinarily exercised indirectly, and the forms of election are observed. For example, when the Chairman of the *raiispolkom* is to be elected, the Bureau of the *raikom* recommends the candidate it favours, who will, in the normal course of events, be nominated at a meeting of the *raion* Soviet. The knowledge that he is the choice of the Party group in the Soviet and enjoys the approval of the *raikom* will usually ensure the nominee's unanimous and unopposed election. A similar procedure will be adopted in filling other elective posts, such as the chairmanships of collective farms and trade union councils.

From time to time, however, instances appear in the Party Press of what may happen when resistance is offered to the *raikom*'s wishes. Thus an editorial article in one Party journal revealed how, at the election of the bureau of a primary oganisation, the *raikom* representative resorted to arbitrary and strictly illegal methods to force the election of the *raikom*'s favoured candidate for the secretaryship even after he had been twice rejected in the voting.[65] In a letter to the same journal a *raikom* propagandist, delegated to represent the *raikom* at the election of a primary organisation Secretary, complained that he had been subsequently accused by the *raikom* and its bureau of 'lack of principle' in not insisting on the re-election of the previous Secretary (who enjoyed the *raikom*'s support but who was morally discredited among the members of the primary organisation) and 'permitting' the election of another comrade in his place.[66]

The major part of the activity of the *raion* and city Party organisation is bound up with supervision and guidance of the

[126]

primary organisations in their areas. In this the Secretaries operate through the permanent staff of instructors in the apparatus, which usually includes at this level organisational, propaganda and agitation and industrial-transport departments. Their functions include political instruction of the primary organisations, organising the fulfilment of Party directives, disseminating experience of Party work and advising on methods of overcoming production problems. In discharging their responsibilities they are required to spend most of their time in direct contact with the members of the primary organisations.[67]

The instructors are supposed to apply the method of helpful persuasion as opposed to issuing orders (*komandovanie*);[68] but there is strong evidence that in this, as in most other aspects of Party supervision, the pressure to achieve rapid economic results (and the bureaucratic behaviour of some local Party officials) often produce the reverse effect. The most frequently voiced complaint of primary organisation Secretaries against *raikoms* and *obkoms* is that they are too remote: they tend to issue written instructions and are not in close enough contact with production and its immediate problems. The turnover of Secretaries of primary organisations is said to be very high—about half of those in Chelyabinsk and Grozny *oblasts* were replaced in 1955—and the cause is seen in the tendency of the *raikom* or *gorkom* to regard them only as 'mechanical executors of orders from above'. Certain *raikoms*, it is stated, 'understand guidance to mean the petty regulating of a Secretary's every step'. The bureau of one *raikom* in the Sumy *oblast* was said to have obliged all the primary organisations in its area to discuss 15, and some organisations 26, of the *raikom*'s decisions during six months of 1956.[69] The First Secretary of one *raikom* was said to have forbidden the holding of Party meetings by primary organisations without his personal sanction.[70]

While the city and *raion* Party organisations exercise supervision over the economic, administrative and cultural life of their respective areas, their jurisdiction does not extend to Party organisations in units of the Armed Forces stationed in those areas. Though required to maintain close contact with local territorial Party committees, these have their own independent channels of command. They work, on the basis of special instructions confirmed by the Central Committee, under the guidance of the Chief Political Administration of the Soviet Army and

Navy which operates as a department of the Central Committee. (Statutes, Articles, 65–67.)

Further statutory functions of the *raion* and city Party organisations are the control of admissions and expulsions from the Party and the maintenance of a register of all Party members and candidate-members in their area. No new member can be admitted into the Party without the formal approval of the bureau of the *raikom* or, in towns without a *raion* division, of the *gorkom*, to which proposals for membership are submitted by Secretaries of primary organisations (Article 4b of Party Statutes). Expulsion from the Party is considered by the general meeting of the appropriate primary organisation, whose decision must be confirmed by the *raikom* or *gorkom* (Article 10). Appeals against expulsion may be lodged both with the Republic Central Committee and with the Party Control Committee of the Central Committee of the CPSU.[71]

The *raikom* and *gorkom* are also the basic Party record offices. They hold a record card for every member and candidate-member in the area, which should provide a complete and up-to-date dossier on his personal, occupational and Party affairs, including changes in employment, education, awards, knowledge of languages, penalties, etc. Among the more sensitive items of information which are required to be entered into a member's Party documents under a Central Committee Instruction of 1956 are: the occupation of the member's parents before and after 1917 (in the case of parents who lived in (*a*) the Baltic States or the Western *oblasts* of the Ukraine and Byelorussia or (*b*) the Tuva Autonomous *oblast*, up to the time of their incorporation into the USSR, the corresponding dates are (*a*) 1940 and (*b*) 1944); in the case of a newly-enrolled member who belonged previously to the CPSU, an indication of the reasons for his earlier departure or expulsion from the Party; and detailed information concerning any past participation in 'oppositions and anti-Party groupings'.[72] All entries in the record cards must be made in a special ink, and the cards must be kept in iron cupboards or safes. *Gorkoms* and *Raikoms* must regularly send statistics on Party membership to higher Party Committees, and on the basis of these Republic Central Committees provide statistics for the CPSU Central Committee. Transfers of Communists from district to district are strictly regulated by Party instructions.[73] A Communist may not transfer without the permission of the Committee where he is registered. If permission is granted his record card must be despatched within seven days by the 'special communications' of the Ministry of Communications to the Party Committee to which he is transferring. He must report to this Committee the day after his arrival and hand in to it a 'de-registration chit'. It is stated to be the duty of *raikom* and *gorkom* Secretaries to interview personally Communists who are being enrolled or removed from the register, but this requirement is not always observed.

PRIMARY ORGANISATIONS

Below the level of the *raion* and city Party organisations are the primary organisations, of which there were stated in 1966 to be 335,000 throughout the country.[74] These are formed at places of work or residence where there are not less than three Party members. Primary organisations are confirmed by the *raikom* or *gorkom* (Statutes, Articles 50, 53).

In factories, offices, etc., where there are over 50 Party members or candidate-members, separate departmental, section or workshop Party organisations may be formed, with the permission of the *raikom* or *gorkom*, within the general primary organisation covering the whole factory, etc. Within these, as within primary organisations with under 50 Party members or candidates, Party groups may be formed in the brigades or units of the establishment. Where there are over 300 members and candidates in factories (over 100 in special cases), or over 50 in collective or state farms, a Party committee for the whole factory or farm may be formed, given the approval in each case of the *oblast* committee (*obkom*), *krai* committee (*kraikom*) or central committee of the Republic Party, with the workshop organisations having the right of primary organisations (Articles 54, 57).

The highest organ of a primary Party organisation is the general meeting of its members, which is required to be held at least once a month or once in two months in the case of organisations having workshop organisations within them. Large organisations with a membership of over 300 hold meetings 'when necessary', as decided by the Committee, or on the demand of several of the workshop organisations. For the conduct of their current business primary organisations having 15 or more members elect a bureau for one year. All, irrespective of size, have a secretary and deputy secretary. If the organisation has no more than 150 members the secretaries combine their Party duties with their ordinary employment; if it has over 150 members they may be full-time paid Party officials. They must in either case have a Party standing of not less than one year (Statutes, Article 56). The Party Committees of large organisations with over 1,000 members may be granted the status of *raikom* (by the Central Committee of a Republic Party) for the purposes of dealing with admissions to the Party, the registration of Party members and personal cases. Party Committees, in such cases, are elected for two years, not one. (Statutes, Article 58).

The tasks of the primary Party organisation, which 'conducts its work directly among the working people, rallies them round the CPSU, and organises the masses to carry out Party policy', are enumerated in the Statutes (Article 59). It:

'(a) admits new members to the CPSU;
(b) educates Communists in a spirit of loyalty to the Party cause . . .;
(c) organises the study by Communists of Marxist-Leninist theory . . . and opposes all attempts at revisionist distortions of Marxism-Leninism and its dogmatic interpretation;
(d) ensures the vanguard rôle of Communists in the sphere of labour and in the socio-political and economic activities of enterprises, collective farms, institutions, educational establishments, etc.;
(e) acts as the organiser of the working people for the performance of the current tasks of Communist construction . . .;
(f) conducts agitational and propaganda work among the masses;
(g) on the basis of extensive criticism and self-criticism, combats cases of bureaucracy, parochialism, and violations of State discipline . . .;
(h) assists the *okrug*, town and *raion* committees in their activities and is accountable to them for its work.'

As part of their control functions in production and trading establishments primary organisations have the statutory right to supervise the activities of the management (Article 60). They have no power, however, to change the production targets of enterprises, which are set by higher authority, and they are warned against usurping the functions of the management and thus violating the principles of 'one-man management' (*edinonachalie*).[75] Their major responsibility appears to be to aid the management in the carrying out of official directives, to use their influence in achieving the fulfilment of plan targets, to develop 'Socialist competition', to discover inadequacies in the work of the enterprise and to recommend remedial measures to the management, and to report to their Party superiors on the state of affairs in the enterprise. From the management they receive periodical reports informing them of problems and developments.[76]

In the State apparatus the work of primary organisations takes a somewhat different form. The Statutes (Article 60) state that 'The Party organisations at Ministries, State Committees and other central and local Soviet or economic agencies and departments which do not have the function of controlling the administration, must actively promote improvement of the apparatus, cultivate among the personnel a high sense of responsibility for work entrusted to them, promote State discipline and the better servicing of the population, firmly combat bureaucracy and red tape, inform the appropriate Party bodies in good time on shortcomings in the work of the respective offices and individuals, regardless of what posts the latter may occupy.' Despite its prominence in the Party Statutes, this distinction of function in enterprises and Soviet institutions appears to be a fine one, and, though the practice is officially condemned, it would appear to be not uncommon for primary organisations in Government institutions to issue direct orders to departmental heads.[77] This can perhaps be partly explained by the fact that the lack of the right of supervision 'does not exempt Communists from responsibility for the state of affairs in the Ministry. They must daily delve into the work of the apparatus'. It is suggested that the duty of the primary organisation in a State institution to signal shortcomings is too often given a 'purely formal interpretation' and that 'signalling is understood in too narrow a sense'. It should not be taken to preclude the 'taking of measures to eliminate the shortcomings'.[78]

A further device for the spreading of Party influence and control is the institution of Party groups in non-Party organisations (Statutes, Articles 68–9). These are set up, when there are not less than three Party members, at all conferences and congresses for the period of the session and, for the full period of election, in all elective bodies of Soviet, trade union, co-operative and other mass organisations. They are subordinate to the corresponding Party organisations (*i.e.* Party groups in the *raion* Soviet or its Executive Committee are directed by the Party *raikom*, a Party group in a factory Trade Union Committee by the factory Party organisation) and they must in all matters abide strictly by the decisions of the leading Party organs.

Their task is to strengthen the Party's influence and to carry out its policy among non-Party people, to stiffen Party and State discipline, combat bureaucracy and check on the fulfilment of Party and Soviet directives. Each Party group elects by open ballot a secretary to deal with current business, and meetings are held whenever necessary. The groups' main tactical purpose is to ensure in advance a single line of conduct for all Communists when agenda items come up for decision and, in this way, to maximise Party influence. They have a purely *ad hoc* status, however, and cannot exercise the functions of primary organisations (such as discussing questions of admission to Party membership, etc.); nor is there any inter-subordination as between Party groups (*e.g.* the Party group in a Soviet is not subordinate to the Party group in its Executive Committee).[79]

SOURCES

1. *Pravda*, October 1, 1965.
2. *XXIII S'ezd KPSS*, Vol. 1, p. 279.
3. *Ibid.*, pp. 9–15.
4. *XX S'ezd KPSS*, Vol. 1, pp. 402, 498.
5. *KPSS v Rezolyutsiyakh*, 1953, Part I, p. 403.
6. *Ibid.*, p. 442.
7. *Ibid.*, p. 525.
8. *Ibid.*, Vol. II, p. 781.
9. *The Dethronement of Stalin*, p. 10.
10. *KPSS v Rezolyutsiyakh*, 1953, Part II, p. 1018.
11. *Ibid.*, p. 1045.
12. Brezhnev's speech at the 1964 October Revolution Anniversary, *Pravda*, November 7, 1964.
13. *Ibid.*
14. *Pravda*, January 15, 1956.
15. *Pravda*, April 18, 1956.
16. *Pravda*, July 2, 1956.
17. *Spravochnik Partiinogo Rabotnika*, p. 336.
18. V. N. Malin *et al.*, p. 381.
19. Longo L. *et al.*, p. 75.
20. *KPSS v Rezolyutsiyakh*, 1953, Part I, p. 443.
21. *Ibid.*
22. Lenin, *Sochineniya*, Vol. 30, p. 413.
23. *The Dethronement of Stalin*, p. 9.
24. *Ibid.*, pp. 31–32.
25. *Ibid.*, p. 32.
26. Lenin, *Sochineniya*, Vol. 32, p. 153.
27. *Pravda*, March 7, 1953.
28. *Pravda*, May 14, 1957.
29. *KPSS v Rezolyutsiyakh*, 1953, Part I, p. 443.
30. *Ibid.*, p. 500.
31. *Pravda*, October 13, 1952.
32. *KPSS v Rezolyutsiyakh*, 1953, Part II, p. 930.
33. *Ibid.*, p. 1129.
34. *XX S'ezd KPSS*, Vol. II, p. 428.
35. *KPSS v Rezolyutsiyak*, 1953, Part II, pp. 779, 929.

36. Longo L. *et al.*, *Problemi e Realtà Dell' URSS*.
37. Longo L. *et al.*, pp. 46–47.
38. *Ibid.*, p. 47.
39. *Ibid.*
40. *Ibid.*, p. 50.
41. *Ibid.*, p. 51.
42. *Ibid.*, p. 52.
43. *Ibid.*, pp. 52–53.
44. *Partiinaya Zhizn*, No. 11, 1957, p. 41.
45. *Partiinaya Zhizn*, No. 15, 1963, pp. 22–3.
46. Longo L. *et al.*, pp. 193–194, 196.
47. *Ibid.*, p. 300.
48. *Ibid.*, p. 216.
49. *Ibid.*, p. 320.
50. *Ibid.*, p. 53.
51. V. N. Malin *et al.*, p. 441; *Partiinaya Zhizn*, No. 11, 1957, p. 40.
52. *Partiinaya Zhizn*, No. 10, 1955, p. 39.
53. *Ibid.*, No. 3, 1954, p. 47; No. 9, 1955, p. 36; No. 10, 1955, pp. 39–40.
54. *XX S'ezd KPSS*, Vol. II, p. 428.
55. *Partiinaya Zhizn*, No. 12, 1955, p. 68.
56. *Moskovskaya Pravda*, March 6, 1966.
57. Longo L. *et al.*, pp. 192–3.
58. *Ibid.*, p. 300.
59. *Ibid.*, pp. 216–217.
60. *Partiinaya Zhizn*, No. 12, 1955, p. 68.
61. *Ibid.*, p. 67.
62. *Ibid.*, No. 20, 1958, p. 48.
63. *Ibid.*, No. 16, 1956, pp. 61–62.
64. *Ibid.*, No. 6, 1958, p. 37.
65. *Ibid.*, No. 23, 1957, p. 70.
66. *Ibid.*, No. 15, 1955, p. 60.
67. *Ibid.*, No. 3, 1957, p. 15ff.
68. *Ibid.*, p. 15.
69. *Ibid.*, No. 18, 1956, pp. 5–6.
70. *Ibid.*, No. 23, 1957, pp. 6–7.
71. *Kommunist*, No. 8, 1957, p. 71 (article by Boitsov).
72. V. N. Malin *et al.*, pp. 420 and 423.
73. *Sputnik Partiinogo Aktivista*, pp. 35–51.
74. *Pravda*, October 25, 1966.
75. L. Slepov, p. 35; A. Petrova *et al.*, p. 27.
76. *Pravda*, October 20, 1954 (article by Vladimirov).
77. A. Petrova *et al.*, p. 206.
78. *Partiinaya Zhizn*, No. 15, 1958, p. 19.
79. *Ibid.*, No. 6, 1955, p. 60.

IX

The Party and the State Administration

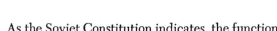

As the Soviet Constitution indicates, the function of the Party in the Soviet State is comprehensive and its concern extends to the whole life of Soviet society. Policy-making is the prerogative of the Party, and the State apparatus exists only to execute its political and economic decisions. This applies, as the Secretary of the Supreme Soviet has declared, even to the 'supreme organ of State power':

'The many-faceted activity of the Supreme Soviet of the USSR is wholly subordinated to ensuring State guidance of the carrying out of the tasks which are worked out by the Communist Party—the leading and directing force of Soviet society.'[1]

The approved method of Party direction of State organs was laid down in a resolution of the 8th Party Congress in 1919. This declared: 'In no event should the functions of Party collectives be confused with the function of the State organs, which are the Soviets. ... The Party must carry out its decisions *via* the Soviet organs, *within the framework of the Soviet Constitution*. The Party tries to *direct* the activity of the Soviets, but not to replace them.'[2] The point is also emphasised in the Party Statutes (Article 42c):

'Party organisations must not act in place of Soviet, trade-union, cooperative or other public organisations ... they must not allow either the merging of the functions of Party and other bodies or undue parallelism in work.'

The fact that these injunctions are constantly reiterated in the Party Press is alone an indication that the 'Party line on the clear distinction of functions between Party and Soviet organs is frequently violated.'[3]

The theoretical position has been clearly set forth in the political organ of the Central Committee:

'Party organisations are not adapted, either by their character or by

their composition, to the fulfilment of the functions of direct administration of the economy. Their duty is to direct and control the work
of Soviet institutions and economic organs in the guidance of industry, agriculture and culture, but not to replace them. . . . By con-
centrating in their hands the decision of all current economic questions, including minor ones, Party committees would inevitably lose
those qualities which are peculiar to them as organs of political and
organisational guidance and would weaken their work among the
masses.'[4]

From this it must obviously be inferred that the carrying out
of Soviet administrative functions by Party organs is to be
deplored not so much as being constitutionally illegal, which it
is, but because it is inexpedient from the point of view of the
Party's effectiveness. There is confirmation of this in an article
in another authoritative journal, which asserts that Party officials
who 'deprive the Soviets of a sense of personal responsibility by
acting over their heads' do so 'in violation of *Party principles* of
leadership' (italics inserted).

Instances of the usurping of Soviet functions by Party officials,
however, are not hard to find, since they continue to be referred
to year after year in the Soviet Press. In 1956 the Smolensk
gorkom was stated to be issuing direct orders concerning matters
—such as street cleaning—which were the direct responsibility
of the *gorispolkom*.[5] In 1957, a *raikom* in the Minsk *oblast* was
stated to have fulfilled until recently all the administrative functions of the *raiispolkom*, whose duties 'boiled down merely to
formalising from a technical point of view what had been
decided by the Party committee'.[6] The *raikom* was still in the
habit of issuing decisions which differed in no way from the
decrees adopted by the *raiispolkom*.[7] And in 1966, 'one still en-
counters cases where a *raikom* or *gorkom* directly replaces economic and Soviet organs. This seriously harms the work of these
organs, reduces their responsibility for the state of affairs in their
area, and has a negative influence on the training of *cadres*.'[8]

It appears to matter little in practice if an order is signed by
the local Party Secretary instead of the Secretary of the *ispolkom*; and whether it has the same legal force is a question
which seems rarely to arise. It was announced at the end of
1957 that by a decree of the Bureau of the Central Committee
of the Communist Party of Georgia the Chairman of the Daesi
Village Soviet in the Kaspi *raion* had been 'dismissed from his
work and expelled from the Party for issuing false documents'.[9]
The power of the Republic Central Committee not only to

impose a Party penalty but to usurp the prerogative of the village Soviet in dismissing its Chairman was not questioned. When such an action appears too blatant, however, and threatens to discredit the Party it may occasionally provoke official criticism. The dismissal of the Chairman of a *gorispolkom* by the bureau of the Molotov *obkom* in 1956 was declared irregular; moreover, it was implied, the same result could have been achieved by observance of the constitutional procedure. 'Of course', it was stated, 'the question of the replacement of the Chairman will in the final analysis be raised at the session of the Soviet, but this is usually done in such a way that everybody can see that the matter is not decided but merely formalised by the Soviet.'[18] The quality most valued in a Party functionary therefore is tact, coupled with the ability to achieve the desired result.

Fundamentally the task of local Party organisations is to adapt central policy to local conditions, and it is through them that the Soviets receive their 'directing instructions'. It is suggested, however, that their guidance of the Soviets be effected 'not by commanding but on the basis of the influence exerted on the activities of these organisations by the Communists working in them.'[11] Since instructions received from higher Party authority are of the same obligatory nature as military orders, however, this influence can hardly be left to individual conscience and public spirit. The minor danger involved in failure to observe the constitutional niceties is no doubt regarded by local Party Committees as infinitely preferable to the major risk incurred by failure to implement policy ordained from above; and it is broadly speaking this consideration that makes direct interference in the administrative functions of Soviets an endemic feature of the work of local Party organisations.

Their guidance of economic organs inevitably confronts them with a similar dilemma. 'Party Committees as organs of political leadership', stated the Party's central newspaper in January, 1955, 'are responsible for the condition of the economy. The Party appraises the work of its local organs on the basis of actual economic results.' Lest this be taken as an invitation to direct intervention, however, it added that 'the solution of economic tasks should be approached with the methods characteristic of Party organisations. Party workers cannot limit their activity to the sphere of economics alone; they are first and foremost social and political workers. What is demanded of them is the ability to combine economic and political work',[12] *i.e.* the formation of right views. In his report to the 20th Congress Khrushchev similarly insisted that Party workers should not separate 'Party work' from 'economic work' but added the warning that this did not imply 'confusion of the functions of Party organs with the functions of economic organs or the replacement of economic organs by Party organs.'[13]

The problem facing Party officials of avoiding charges on the one hand of indifference to their economic responsibilities and on the other of excessive interference with management is not easily resolved. Their effectiveness is judged on the basis of economic achievement in their own area. Indeed at the 20th Congress Khrushchev even suggested, on the grounds that Party-organisational work can be considered successful only 'if it tells positively on production', that their salaries should also be made dependent on economic success.[14] It is this fact of being held to account for the success or failure of the economic agencies in their area that impels some Party functionaries to assume operational supervision over them. Since, moreover, both they and the managerial personnel share the responsibility for economic results, there has developed a mutual dependency which can lead, as was pointed out earlier, to either bribery or an agreement to refrain from mutual criticism. In a case reported in 1954, for example, the secretary of the Party organisation in the USSR Ministry of Construction was found to have been given the fictitious but paid post of deputy-minister: 'Minister Dygai', it was stated, 'irresponsibly fixed rates of payment to Party officials and by thus corrupting them tied their hands'.[15]

There have been indications of an attempt to enhance the rôle of the Party organisations in the State apparatus in connection with the reform of industrial administration introduced by the post-Khrushchev régime. At the end of 1966 the Party Central Committee held a seminar for secretaries of Party organisations in Ministerial and other Governmental offices at which they were told it was quite wrong to think that these Party organisations had only limited possibilities for exerting their influence, and were reminded of their duty to report on shortcomings in the work of offices and individuals, 'regardless of what posts the latter may occupy'.[16]

Theoretically, Party control of administrative and economic bodies is exerted indirectly, through the Communists who work in them; and staffing ('cadres work') has therefore been from the first a principal concern of the Party. 'Correct guidance of Soviets by Party committees', it is said, 'primarily consists in strengthening Soviet organs with experienced and trained workers, possessing initiative and capable of carrying out in practice the Party line.'[17] What this frequently means in practice, as has already been seen, is that many of the local Party and Soviet leaders are the same. The first secretary of the Party Committee is normally a member of the Soviet executive committee, and the chairman of the Soviet executive committee is usually a member of the Party bureau. A Party journal declared in 1956 that, as a result of this interlocking of Party and Soviet deliberative bodies, 'in the recent past . . . leading workers of the *oblast* and *raions* spent almost the whole time at meetings. Scarcely had a meeting of the bureau of the *obkom*, lasting many hours and frequently many days, come to an end, when a meeting of the Soviet *ispolkom* began.'[18] This situation had been improved, it was claimed, by the reduction in the number of meetings; but it seemed that it remained usual for local leading officials to serve in both bodies. The doctrinal justification for this exists, in any case, in Lenin's dictum on the merging of the 'upper strata' of the Soviets with those of the Party,[19] which was later developed by Stalin in his much-quoted statement to the 18th Party Congress to the effect that the Party cadres 'constitute the commanding staff of the Party; and since our Party is in power they also constitute the commanding staff of the leading State organs'.[20] The identification of Party and State leaders at top level has already been referred to.

Cadres work may perhaps be defined as the placing of the right people in the right positions of authority and inducing in them a sense of responsibility for seeing that Party directives are efficiently carried out. The area of responsibility of Party organisations in this matter is defined by the schedule of appointments (*nomenklatura*) which is allocated to the Party Committee at each level and for which it is responsible as the appointing or confirming authority. These may include, in addition to elective posts in local Party organisations, Soviets, trade union councils, etc., those of leading officials in collective farms, procurement agencies, etc., and of managerial and technical staff in factories and other key personnel. While the size of the *nomenklatura* will naturally vary with the region, there have been indications that in the case of the rural *raion* it has included some hundreds of types of posts and in the union republic some thousands.[21] The *nomenklatura* of the Party committee of a smaller, urban *raion* was said in 1958 to include 67 posts.[22] The allocation of responsibility for specific appointments may vary with time and place depending on their current importance. Thus it appears that until early 1954 responsibility for the appointment of collective farm chairmen lay with the *raikom*. A Central Committee decree of March 2, 1954, however, stated that 'for the purpose of enhancing the responsibility of local Party organisations for the correct selection, placing and education of leading collective farm cadres', such appointments were to be transferred to the *nomenklatura* of the *obkom*, while the *raikom's* responsibility extended only to the posts of deputy chairmen, leaders of work brigades and managers of livestock farms.[23]

In the economic sphere a Party committee's main effort should, it seems, be directed towards providing for the local industry a sufficient nucleus of reliable people to ensure fulfilment of the Party's economic directives. This is particularly the case with agriculture, in which the Party's responsibility became of a peculiarly direct administrative kind under Khrushchev. Thus in 1956 it was stated that certain *raikoms* in the Smolensk *oblast* were not doing enough to increase the number of Communists engaged in livestock farming, the crisis sector of Soviet agriculture: 'In the Semlevo *raion* only two Communists are engaged in livestock farming; in Tumanovo *raion*, six; in *Znamenka* raion, nine. It is understandable that with such an insignificant Party substratum it is difficult to achieve the proper development of livestock farming.'[24]

The Party is not the sole agency in the selection and recommending of personnel. In appointments other than those of its own staff it shares its responsibility with other organs. Both ministries and enterprises have their own cadres departments, while appointments to elective posts require the formal sanction of the representative body, whether a Soviet or a general meeting of collective farmers. As the 'leading nucleus' of all such bodies, however, the Party bears the greatest responsibility and authority, and in practice its recommendations can rarely be challenged, even if they are privately disputed. As the secretary of one *raikom* was able to claim of the time when collective farm chairmanships were included in its *nomenklatura*, 'the *raikom's* recommendations always received the unanimous support of the collective farmers'.[25]

In the Party mind economic, political and ideological work are closely interlinked. Life in the Soviet Union is mainly conceived in economic terms, and in definitions of the Party's work the economic motive predominates. The subject of the Party's vast and all-embracing scheme of propaganda and agitation is outside the scope of this study, but it should perhaps be stressed in the present context that one of its main and continuing purposes as a political instrument is to boost the country's economic potential by promoting correct attitudes among the masses, by inducing conformity of thought and action. 'Agitational-propagandist and all ideological work', the Party functionary is constantly reminded, 'is designed to help the more successful solution of production tasks.'[26]

SOURCES

1. *Sovety Deputatov Trudyash-chikhsya*, No. 1, 1958, p. 15 (article by M. Georgadze).
2. *KPSS v Rezolyutsiyakh*, 1953, Part I, p. 446.
3. *Kommunist*, No. 17, 1956, p. 15.
4. *Ibid.*, p. 14.
5. *Ibid.*, p. 15.
6. *Partiinaya Zhizn*, No. 3, 1957, pp. 59–60.
7. *Ibid.*, p. 61.
8. *Partiinaya Zhizn*, No. 15, 1966, p. 15.
9. *Zarya Vostoka*, December 24, 1957.
10. *Partiinaya Zhizn*, No. 20, 1956, p. 54.
11. *Sovetskoe Gosudarstvo i Pravo*, No. 12, 1947, p. 10 (article by V. Borisov).
12. *Pravda*, January 5, 1955.
13. *Pravda*, February 15, 1956.
14. *Ibid.*
15. *Partiinaya Zhizn*, No. 3, 1954, p. 48.
16. *Partiinaya Zhizn*, No. 24, 1966, p. 29; *Pravda*, December 30, 1966.
17. *Partiinaya Zhizn*, No. 2, 1957, p. 8.
18. *Kommunist*, No. 3, 1956, p. 63 (article by P. Doronin).
19. Lenin, *Sochineniya*, Vol. 31, p. 153.
20. Stalin, *Problems of Leninism*, p. 784.
21. D. J. R. Scott, p. 182.
22. *Partiinaya Zhizn*, No. 13, 1958, p. 10.
23. *Pravda*, March 6, 1954.
24. *Kommunist*, No. 3, 1956, p. 65.
25. A. Krivoshei, *Glavnoe—V Organizatorskoi Rabote*, p. 8.
26. *Partiinaya Zhizn*, No. 21, 1955, p. 6.

BIBLIOGRAPHY

Ananov, I. N., *Ministerstva v SSSR* (Ministries in the USSR), State Publishing House of Juridical Literature, Moscow, 1960.

Askerov, A. A., *et al.* (compilers), *Sovetskoe Gosudarstvennoe Pravo* (Soviet State Law) Juridical Publishing House of the Ministry of Justice of the USSR, Moscow, 1948.

Bakinsk:· Rabochii (Baku Worker), newspaper of the Azerbaidjan Party Central Committee, Supreme Soviet and Council of Ministers.

Bolshaya Sovetskaya Entsiklopediya (Large Soviet Encyclopaedia), 1st edition, 65 volumes with supplementary volume on the USSR, Moscow, 1926–47; 2nd edition, 51 volumes with supplementary volume on the USSR, Moscow, 1949–58. (Cited as B.S.E.)

Bolshevik (Bolshevik), now *Kommunist* (Communist), periodical, organ of the Central Committee of the Communist Party of the Soviet Union.

Byulleten Ispolnitelnogo Komiteta Moskovskogo Gorodskoga Soveta Deputatov Trudyashchikhsya (Bulletin of Executive Committee of the Moscow City Soviet).

Chkhikvadze, V. M., et al., *Slovar Pravovykh Znanii* (Dictionary of Legal Knowledge), Soviet Encyclopaedia Publishing House, Moscow, 1965.

Denisov, A. L., *Vysshie Organy Gosudarstvennoi Vlasti i Organy Gosuderstvennogo Upravleniya SSSR* (Higher Organs of State Power and Organs of State Administration of the USSR), Publishing House of the Gazette of the Supreme Soviet of the RSFSR, Moscow, 1941.

Dethronement of Stalin, Khrushchev's 'Secret' speech to the 20th Party Congress, issued as a pamphlet by the *Manchester Guardian*, June, 1956.

Filonovich, Yu K., *Sovetsky Deputat* (The Soviet Deputy), State Publishing House of Juridical Literature, Moscow, 1958.

Gsovski, V., *Soviet Civil Law* (2 volumes), University of Michigan Law School, 1948.

Il Messaggero, Rome independent newspaper.

Izvestiya (News), newspaper of the Presidium of the USSR Supreme Soviet.

Kommunist (Communist) newspaper of the Armenian Party Central Committee, Supreme Soviet and Council of Ministers.

Kommunist (Communist), formerly *Bolshevik*, periodical published by the Central Committeee of the Communist Party of the Soviet Union.

KPSS v Rezolyutsiyakh i Resheniyakh S'ezdov, Konferentsii i Plenumov Ts.K. (The CPSU in Resolutions and Decisions of Congresses, Conferences and Plenums of the C.C.), 7th edition, 2 volumes, State Publishing House of Political Literature, Moscow, 1953.

Krasnaya Zvezda (Red Star), newspaper of the Ministry of Defence of the USSR.

Kravtsov, B. P., *Sovetskaya Izbiratelnaya Sistema* (The Soviet Electoral System), State Publishing House of Juridical Literature, Moscow, 1957.

Kravtsov, B. P., *Verkhovny Sovet SSSR* (The Supreme Soviet of the USSR), State Publishing House of Juridical Literature, Moscow, 1954.

Krivoshei, A., *Glavnoye—v Organizatorskoi Rabote* (The Main Thing is Organisational Work), State Publishing House of Political Literature, Moscow, 1956.

Lenin, V. I., *Sochineniya* (works), 3rd edition, 30 volumes, Publishing House of the Central Committee of the VKP (b).

Lenin, V. I., *Sochineniya* (works), 4th edition, 35 volumes, Marx-Engels-Lenin Institute, Moscow, 1941–50.

Lipatov, A. A., and Savenkov, N. T. (compilers), *Istoriya Sovetskoi Konstitutsii, 1917–56* (The History of the Soviet Constitution 1917–56), State Publishing House of Juridical Literature, Moscow, 1957.

Longo, L., *et al.*, *Problemi e Realtà dell'URSS*, Editori Riuniti, Rome, 1958.

Luzhin, A. V., *Gorodskie Sovety Deputatov Trudyashchikhsya* (Town Soviets), State Publishing House of Juridical Literature, Moscow, 1954.

Luzhin, A. V., *Postoyannye Komissii Mestnykh Sovetov Deputatov Trudyashchikhsya* (Permanent Commissions of Local Soviets), State Publishing House of Juridical Literature, Moscow, 1953.

Malin, V. N., *et al.*, *Spravochnik Partiinogo Rabotnika* (Party Worker's Handbook), State Publishing House of Political Literature, Moscow, 1957.

Mamontov, I., *Nerushimy Blok Kommunistov i Bespartiinykh* (The Indestructible Block of Communists and Non-Party People), State Publishing House of Political Literature, Moscow, 1954.

Moscovskaya Pravda, Newspaper of the Moscow Party Committee and the Moscow Soviet.

New Times, weekly, published by *Trud* (Labour), Moscow.

[142]

Novikov, S. G., *Postoyannye Komissii Verkhovnogo Soveta SSSR* (Permanent Commissions of Supreme Soviet of USSR), State Publishing House of Juridical Literature, Moscow, 1958.

Osnovy Sovetskogo Gosudarstvennogo Stroitelstva i Prava (The Bases of Soviet State Construction and Law), *Mysl* Publishing House, Moscow, 1965.

Partiinaya Zhizn (Party Life), periodical published by the Central Committee of the Communist Party of the Soviet Union.

Petrov, G. I., (compiler), *Osnovy Sovetskogo Gosudarstvennogo Prava i Sovetskoe Stroitelstvo* (The Bases of Soviet Constitutional Law and Soviet Construction), *Lenizdat* Publishing House, Leningrad, 1961.

Petrova, A., *et al.*, *Pervichnaya Partiinaya Organizatsiya* (The Primary Party Organisation), *Moskovsky Rabochii* Publishing House, Moscow, 1954.

Planovoe Khozyaistvo (Planned Economy), periodical published by the USSR State Planning Commission.

Polozhenie o Vyborakh v Verkhovny Sovet SSSR (Statute on Elections to Supreme Soviet of USSR), State Publishing House of Juridical Literature, Moscow, 1966.

Pravda (Truth), newspaper, organ of the Central Committee of the Communist Party of the Soviet Union.

Sbornik Zakonov SSSR i Ukazov Prezidiuma Verkhovnogo Soveta SSSR, 1945–46 (Collection of USSR Laws and Edicts of the Presidium of the Supreme Soviet, 1945–46), publication of the 'Gazette of the USSR Supreme Soviet', Moscow, 1947.

Scott, D. J. R., Russian Political Institutions, George Allen & Unwin, London, 1958.

Shapiro, L., The Origin of the Communist Autocracy, G. Bell & Sons, London, 1955.

Slepov, L., *O Stile v Partiinoi Rabote* (On Style in Party Work), State Publishing House of Political Literature, Moscow, 1953.

Sotsialistcheskaya Zakonnost (Socialist Legality), periodical, organ of the Prosecutor's Office of the USSR.

Sovetskaya Latvya (*Soviet Latvia*), newspaper of the Latvian Party Central Committee, Supreme Soviet and Council of Ministers.

Sovetskaya Litva (Soviet Lithuania), newspaper of the Lithuanian Party Central Committee, Supreme Soviet and Council of Ministers.

Sovetskaya Rossiya (Soviet Russia), newspaper of the Central Committee of the Communist Party of the Soviet Union.

Sovetskoe Gosudarstvo i Pravo (Soviet State and Law), periodical published by the Institute of State and Law of the USSR Academy of Sciences.

Sovety Deputatov Trudyashchikhsya (Soviets of Workers' Deputies), periodical, publication of the newspaper *Izvestiya*.

Soviet Weekly, organ of the Soviet Embassy, London.
Spravochnik Partiinogo Rabotnika, 1966. (Party Worker's Handbook, 1966), Publishing House of Political Literature, Moscow, 1966.
Sputnik Partiinogo Aktivista (Party Activist's Companion), Military Publishing House, Moscow, 1965.
Stalin, J. V., *Problems of Leninism*, Foreign Languages Publishing House, Moscow, 1953.
Stalin, J. V., *Works*, 13 volumes, Foreign Language Publishing House, Moscow, 1952.
Starovoitov, N. G., *Demokratism Sovetskoi Konstitutsii* (The Democracy of the Soviet Constitution), State Publishing House of Juridical Literature, Moscow, 1958.

USSR Questions and Answers, Novosti Publishing House, Moscow, No date (1964?).

Vedomosti Verkhovnogo Soveta RSFSR (Gazette of the RSFSR Supreme Soviet), organ of the Supreme Soviet of the RSFSR.
Vedomosti Verkhovnogo Soveta SSSR (Gazette of the USSR Supreme Soviet), organ of the Supreme Soviet of the USSR.
Voprosy Istorii KPSS (Questions of History of the CPSU) periodical, organ of the Institute of Marxism-Leninism attached to the Central Committee of the CPSU.
V Pomoshch Politicheskomu Samoobrazovaniyu (Aid to Political Self-Education, periodical, organ of the Central Committee of the Communist Party of the Soviet Union.
Vyshinsky, A. Ya., Law of the Soviet State, Macmillan Company of New York, 1948.

XX S'ezd KPSS, Stenograficheski Otchet (20th Congress of the CPSU, Stenographic Report), State Publishing House of Political Literature, Moscow, 1956.
XXIII S'ezd KPSS, Stenograficheski Otchet (23rd Congress of the CPSU, Stenographic Report), State Publishing House of Political Literature, Moscow, 1966.

Yampolskaya, Ts. A., *Organy Sovetskogo Gosuderstvennogo Upravleniya* (Organs of Soviet State Administration), Publishing House of the Academy of Sciences of the USSR, Moscow, 1954.

Zarya Vostoka (Dawn of the East), newspaper of the Georgian Party Central Committee, Supreme Soviet and Council of Ministers.
Zasedaniya Verkhovnogo Soveta SSSR Pyatogo Sozyva (Pervaya Sessiya) Stenograficheski Otchet (Meetings of the USSR Supreme Soviet of the Fifth Convocation (First Session), Stenographic Report), Publication of the USSR Supreme Soviet, 1958.

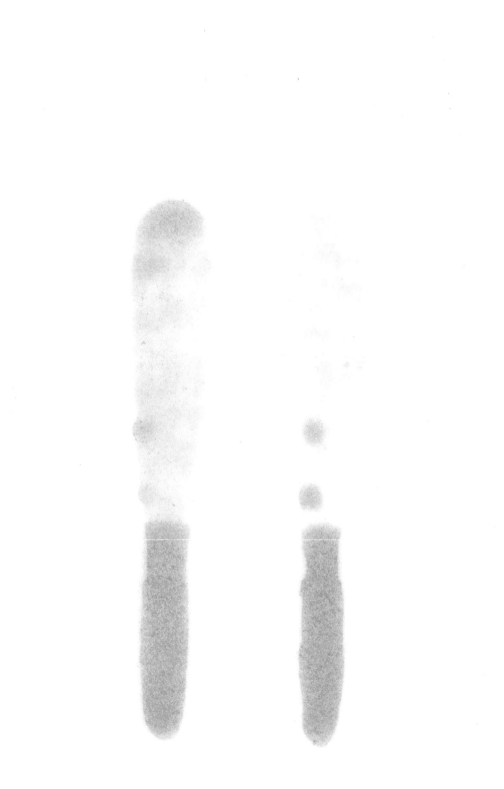

DATE DUE

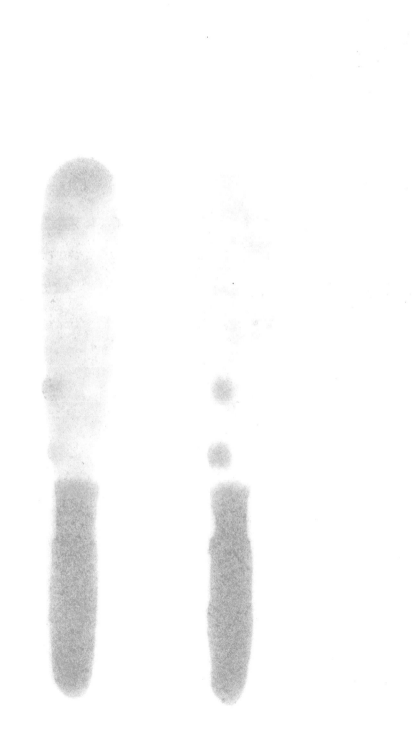

DATE DUE